Write of Passage
Volume II

A Southerner's View of Then and Now

By John Moore

Copyright © 2019 John Moore

Books by John Moore

**Write of Passage
A Southerner's View of Then and Now**

Write of Passage Volume II

John's books are available on Amazon and at
TheCountryWriter.com.

John Moore is an Arkansas native who lives in East Texas where he writes a weekly syndicated column and owns a voiceover recording studio. He spent over two decades in the radio business as a reporter and disc jockey. He and his wife enjoy quiet time on their homestead with their peacock named Fred.

Thanks

This is my second book. Elise and Emmitte edited and steered the first one and hung around to do the same for this edition. I appreciate them both.

The stories in this book are mostly from memory. Any errors are solely mine.

Dedication

For my mom. Who has always had my back.

WRITE OF PASSAGE, VOL. 2

TABLE OF CONTENTS

CHAPTER ONE – School Days

All Y'all

Y'all ever heard of a colloquialism?

According to the folks at Merriam-Webster a colloquialism is "a local or regional dialect expression."

Another definition is using language that could be considered "unacceptably informal."

I have been accused of both. Being unacceptable and informal – sometimes separately, but most often in combination.

Yankees often make fun of Southerners for the way we talk by trying to imitate us. Truth is, there isn't much else that's funnier than someone with a thick Northern accent muddling through saying, "You all," instead of "y'all."

And no, you don't capitalize y'all.

But what the folks up north, and honestly, most of us in the South would be surprised to learn is that the word that is used most often below the Mason-Dixon line, didn't originate in

Tennessee, Texas, Arkansas, or anywhere else where grits and gravy are the standard fare. The word "y'all," can be traced back to the Scots-Irish.

Very few of us are Native American. Virtually all of us are immigrants. My ancestry.com DNA test shows that I'm 69 percent British, but I'm also part Scottish.

So, it makes sense that much of the English language that the Scots-Irish (Scots are the people, Scotch is the drink) brought a mix of different words and dialects to the Ozarks and Appalachia in North America. Down through the centuries, some of these words would become misheard and likely morphed into something other than their original form.

Y'all still with me?

Many languages have two different words for the word, "you." There's one word if you're talking to one person and a different word if you're talking to more than one person.

English used to have the same thing. Look no further than your King James Bible for an example. "Thou" meant "you," and "Ye" was used as the plural. But, there were certain Scottish dialects that used "ye all" as the plural.

When these folks left Europe and wound up in the mountainous areas of what is now America, "ye all" was already part of their language. So, it was heard often.

The Scots-Irish were known as hillbillies but probably not for any of the negative reasons that you might think. More on that in a moment.

Time passed and those who heard their new mountain neighbors talking, quite possibly thought they heard "ya'll" instead of "ye all," but it's also just as likely that over time the Scots-Irish just shortened it on their own.

And "y'all" was born.

Any mash-ups or changes in the language that led us to "y'all," don't alter its meaning.

Without exception, "y'all" is always plural.

When someone says, "Hey, y'all," or "What's up, y'all?" Or "Are y'all fixin' to go to the store?" (see complete details on the phrase, 'fixin' to' in a column y'all need to read when I eventually write it), they are referring to more than one person.

If a Southerner is asking an individual a question, such as inquiring about their overall current sense of wellbeing, they ask, "How you?"

"How y'all?" is when you ask two or more folks about their overall current senses of well-being.

What's even more interesting about the slang that the Scots-Irish used (perfected is the term I prefer), is that those who get the credit for "y'all" were connected to royalty.

The Highland Scots were called, "Hill Folks" by their neighbors. And during the wars of the late 1600s they backed Britain's King William.

Because of this they were called "Billy Boys," which later led to them being called, "Hill Billy Boys." And much like "Ye all" got shortened to "y'all," "Hill Billy Boys" was eventually shortened to "Hillbillies." This term followed them to the US.

Other places where English is spoken have their own version of "y'all." Drive past that last BBQ joint just north of St. Louis and suddenly, "y'all" becomes "you guys." And that's even if a girl is present.

Go figure.

In New Jersey, "youse guys" is the term, unless they're juveniles, then they're "yutes" (see the movie, 'My Cousin Vinnie').

In England, "you lot" is the term for y'all (don't ask me).

Enough of the history lesson. Let's focus on the proper uses for "y'all."

As was mentioned, "y'all" is always plural, unless you're talking about a pretty large group. That's when "y'all" is replaced by "all y'all."

Examples:

If there are two people in front of you, you should ask, "Are y'all going to the Lynyrd Skynyrd concert?"

If there are 317 people in front of you, you should ask, "Are all y'all going to the Lynyrd Skynyrd concert?"

One thing that doesn't enjoy wide agreement is the possessive of "y'all."

Now, I know that's confusing, because "y'all" is plural, but what would plural possessive be?

Should it be "y'alls" or "y'all's"?

Examples:

If you have two people in front of you, you should ask, "Are y'all going to get y'alls Lynyrd Skynyrd concert tickets?"

If you have 319 people in front of you, you should ask, "Are all y'all going to get y'all's Lynyrd Skynyrd concert tickets?"

(Two more people showed up for tickets when they heard that Lynyrd Skynyrd was playing a concert.)

More and more of our northern brethren are moving to the South, so it's important that we do the right thing and reach out to them and offer to help in any way that we can. One way we can help is to offer to translate for them.

Make sure that they understand y'all, all y'all, and y'alls or y'all's (your choice on the last two).

And, if they don't know who Lynyrd Skynyrd is, please put "Sweet Home Alabama" in the disc changer.

All y'all have a good week. I'm fixin' to start my next column.

Tick Tock

I read something recently that was a bit disconcerting. Someone was offering a class to teach children how to tell time.
Think about that.

We've simplified the most basic things to the point where children, the very group of people that we will all rely on to run the country and our nursing homes when we reach old age, can't read a watch or a clock.

Sure, kids, or anyone else for that matter, can look at a cell phone or a digital device and know what time it is. But, they can't read the face of an analog clock.

On the surface, this may seem like no big deal, but this is the latest in a trend of basics that someone, somewhere along the way, decided wasn't important enough for our children to learn.

Children are not being taught the most rudimentary of abilities that we all learned and take for granted.

15

A few years ago, I heard that cursive writing was no longer being taught in schools. I suspected (incorrectly, it seems) that maybe that was a voluntary thing. Now, I'm hearing that kids are being dinged or chastised for using cursive.

My generation was taught typing, which is now called keyboarding. Don't get me wrong, typing is one of the most valuable skill sets I acquired in high school. For young people now, that's no different. But, what happens when the electricity goes off?

There's nothing wrong with printing as a form of writing, but cursive is a much faster means of communication. I can remember spending hours in third and fourth grade practicing cursive. I was never very good at it, and I'm still not, but cursive used to be an art form.

Look at the United States Constitution and the Declaration of Independence. James Madison and Thomas Jefferson, respectively, painstakingly used a quill pen and ink to write out, in cursive, what are two of the most important documents that history has ever seen.

Good penmanship used to be a point of pride, and it was often beautiful.

Computers have not only all but eliminated writing by hand from our kids' list of abilities, they've also all but omitted the need to go to the library. The hours that my age group spent learning the Dewey Decimal System as a pathway to research and expand our knowledge has been replaced by websites that may or may not be reliable sources of information.

A few years ago, I went to our local book repository to sign my wife and myself up for library cards, and even donated some books while I was there. Each time I've visited since, the youngest person there was the lady working the counter.

Young people aren't learning how to find their own information. They rely almost solely on an electronic device and Google. I'm guessing that if you asked someone under age 30 if they could tell you about Funk & Wagnalls, they'd guess that they were a hip-hop group.

Reading a map is also being lost to time. It wasn't so long ago that a trip of any length first required stopping at a Texaco or Shell station to buy road maps or a road atlas of the states that connected you to your destination. Now, people blindly trust some unseen lady named Siri who lives inside our cell phones to tell us where to go, turn and stop.

These same electronic devices have also essentially crippled us, should we actually have to remember someone's phone number. Keeping an address book (in pencil) was once standard in every household. We referenced them for numbers we called infrequently; but most people that we called, we remembered their numbers.

Today, young and old alike simply have to touch the name of the person we want to call on our cell, and we no longer learn, or we have forgotten, their phone number.

We have arrived at a place that is somewhat frightening. Fewer of us know how to do for ourselves. We blindly rely on a system of communication and information that, should someone flip off its switch tomorrow, most of us not only have no backup system, a vast chunk of society wouldn't know how to use it if they did.

The best favor we can do for young people is to show them some basics. Before time runs out.

In A Class Of Our Own

Einstein's theory of relativity includes
something called "time dilation."

I'm about as far from being a scientist as one
can possibly be, but the way that I understand
time dilation, two clocks show different times
when they're affected by gravity or velocity. A
clock on earth would move faster than one in
orbit. The faster you go, the slower time moves.

Supposedly, this theory has been proven
through multiple tests, but my own test also
bears out his results.

As evidence, I present the fact that it seems as if
I just graduated from high school, but the
calendar indicates almost 40 years have passed.

I have never been in orbit, save for a few
unaccounted for evenings in the '70s, yet
Einstein's theory seems valid.

I subscribe to a number of local newspapers,
and recently, as occurs annually, each edition
contained ads and articles congratulating recent
graduates.

I scanned the information under each person's photo. The students, now graduates, were preparing for the next leg of their journey.

I remembered what it was like to be facing that pivotal moment in life.

Graduation night for my classmates and me was hot and muggy. Rain forced us into the un-air-conditioned gymnasium, where I thought about current events instead of listening to our commencement speaker.

1980 was a tumultuous year in America. Those of us standing in that gym wearing our purple caps and gowns were filled with personal uncertainty.

Vietnam was still visible in our collective rear-view mirror; 52 of our fellow citizens were being held hostage in Iran; unemployment and interest rates were rising; and each of us were just minutes away from being foisted into the world, no longer as a class, but as individuals.

I'd doubt that many, if any, of us thought much about it at that moment, but we were about to embark on a path filled with a lot of guesses, guidance, and thankfully God, that would take us to the places we were meant to go.

We would make a lot of mistakes, enjoy a lot of successes, feel the warmth of love, and the pain of loss. It wouldn't be the first time we'd felt any of these things, but it would be the first time we'd felt them without each other.

Many of those I stood with that night, I had also stood with on the first day of school. As Lyndon Johnson was wrapping up his stint in the Oval Office, Henry Platt became one of my first-grade friends. In Mrs. Walker's class, Henry and I learned where the letters that made words came from.

Mother Alphabet.

Mrs. Walker would explain to us at the beginning of a new class that "Mother Alphabet" had had another letter.

Henry and I would take our big, red, Husky pencils and copy down the newest letter onto our Big Chief tablets. Henry always caught on faster than I did when it came to learning to write.

I would go home each day and tell my mom, "Mother Alphabet had another letter today!"

My mom always acted excited, but I'm guessing that she probably was thinking that Father Alphabet needed to take a vacation.

Henry was one of my first friends, but there would be many others over the next dozen years. I can't name every school pal here. I wish I could. What I can say here is that every single classmate of mine shaped, in some way, who I am today.

Jeff Sikes demonstrated that it is possible for a child to be far smarter than most adults, without hurting the adults' feelings.

Adam Cummings became my good friend. He was everything I wasn't. He was cool, athletic, and a girl magnet. But, Adam and I shared a sense of humor and a love of music and cool cars.

Scotty Davis was an entrepreneur before I even knew that word. He and his brother, Andy, were always coming up with some way to make money. Raking leaves, mowing yards, and buying and selling motorcycles were just some of the things I learned could be more than just a quick buck; they could be businesses.

Doug Daniel was the bass player in his and my first rock band.

Steve Scarborough helped me get into my first paying rock band.

Kirk Mounts showed me how to be the John Ritter of the class, before "Three's Company" ever hit the airwaves.

Stanley Nations proved that it was possible for a 10th-grade guy to date a 12th-grade girl.

Lisa Pounds and Tammy Moon were two of my girlfriends. That is how you write that a girl was your friend and not a romantic interest, isn't it?

However, there were a handful of girls in my class who took pity on me and actually went out with me on dates. I'm guessing that they have special rewards waiting in the afterlife.

I'm sure that the recent graduates will one day look back at their time growing up the same way that I do: with clarity. They will see that all along the way, their classmates exhibited much of who they would be as adults.

My friends certainly did.

Henry Platt is now Dr. Henry Platt. Adam had a successful career and was active in his church before a disease took him a few years ago.

Scotty became a successful businessman. Doug works in the paper manufacturing industry. Steve started a printing business. Kirk is now the town treasurer. Stanley is self-employed. The ladies from my class went on to find happiness in business and in life.

Einstein's time dilation got one thing right: Clocks definitely move faster than seems possible here on earth. But, he left out the part about being able to go back in time.

Time travel is as easy as thinking about my classmates. And I visit them quite often.

Old News

As we get older, we see aging in others, but we never age.

At least, we don't see ourselves aging.

I remember going to my 35th high school class reunion a few years ago. A classmate was kind enough to host a gathering at his home for the handful who could make it. Around 30 of my graduating class of about 150 showed up.

It was a typical Arkansas October, so the weather was quite pleasant. The few of us who arrived early set up lawn chairs and coolers in the driveway and on the patio as a makeshift party location and began to reminisce.

As others arrived and got out of their vehicles and started the walk up the drive, in quiet voices we began playing, "Does anyone know who that is?"

This wasn't meant to be funny. People had just changed that much. We didn't recognize them.

When David Cassidy died, I was surprised at his most recent photos. He was an old man.

There was no reason for me to be surprised that Cassidy didn't look like the 21-year-old heartthrob he was almost 50 years ago. He was 67 when he passed away. Old enough for Medicare and Social Security.

But, for whatever reason, the way we remember people is as their younger selves. Perhaps that's the way we want to remember those we've known a long time.

The photos we normally see in obituaries are of the deceased when they were younger.

Sometimes, but not often, a recent photo is used of the person who has passed.

There's just something about youth that's more appealing than aging.

As I've gotten older, more and more I wonder why this is.

Youth does offer a lot. Specifically, it provides stamina, few if any aches or pains, not many cares or burdens, and the rest of your life ahead of you.

But, age brings wisdom. Not that we all use wisdom as wisely as we should. I certainly know that I haven't. Each year we are given is an opportunity to encounter, engage, and resolve problems or issues that come with life. It's also an opportunity to learn from good decisions and mistakes and make better choices going forward.

You would think that age would be held in a higher regard than it is. In some cultures, that's the case. But not in the U.S. Whether it's Hollywood or our own desire to remain ever youthful, we hang onto the idea that we would like to look the same as we did when we were young.

Plastic surgeons live in nice houses because of this. And there's nothing wrong with that. I'm all for folks being left alone and allowed to make their own choices. I have a great amount of admiration for those who embrace getting older and couldn't care less what other people think.

When I was a kid virtually every newscaster on the networks was an older guy. Today, it seems to be all about finding the youngest and most attractive person possible to sit at a news desk.

I'm not passing judgment at all on those who are TV anchors these days. However, I will point out that once upon a time, the most trusted man in America was Walter Cronkite.

Uncle Walter would never have won a beauty contest, but when he told us something we listened. And what was Walter? He was old.

There is a trend in this country to dismiss the older folks. Our culture has raised looking young almost to a level of deification. However, those of us who are middle aged and older have to also point the finger at ourselves.

Singers, actors, and others in the spotlight reach the zenith of their popularity when they are young. It is us who make this so. If you need

27

proof, just look at Burt Reynolds, Robert Redford, and Candice Bergen. Thirty years ago, they were some of the highest-paid actors.

Today, they're almost a memory.

I've had the opportunity more than once to sit down and talk with some volunteers with whom I work who are now in their 60s, 70s, and 80s. Many of them were once high-level corporate executives.

During our conversations, they've talked about how much they enjoy retirement and volunteering. But, they have also discussed some of their accomplishments. When I watch the news and hear about some of the foolish corporate decisions made by younger executives, I have to wonder if a couple of phone calls to one of these older folks might have helped.

There's a place in society for everyone. Youth offers stamina. Age offers wisdom. If each group reached out to the other, both would greatly benefit.

But, we have to force ourselves to focus less on looks and more on what's inside.

CHAPTER TWO – SEEMS LIKE OLD TIMES

Out to The Outhouse

Raise your hand if you've ever used an outhouse.

During a recent discussion with friends, the topic of outhouses came up. I honestly don't remember why it made its way into the conversation, but boy, did it ever.

So, I posed the question on my Facebook page, yes or no, have you ever used an outhouse? I was shocked at not only the number of people who said yes, but also at the number of people who responded with comments about their outhouse experiences.

And for the most part, folks who have used an outhouse are very proud of that fact.

Growing up in rural Arkansas, there were a number of my family members and friends who still lived life much as they always had. In the mid-1960s, I was very young, but many of my great-grandparents were not only still alive, they were still active.

About 1966, my mother's grandparents were homesteading a small farm on Highway 41 between New Boston, Texas and Foreman, Arkansas. The only running water they had in the old farmhouse was a hand pump in the kitchen sink. From there, my great grandmother would draw water for baths, washing clothes, and cooking.

My great-grandparents also had what is called a one-holer outhouse, which, as indicated, is designed for one person at a time. Inside by the door, you would find a nail sticking out with a copy of the Farmer's Almanac hanging from it. Also, nearby would be a Sears and Roebuck catalog. This is because Charmin wasn't readily available at their place.

Outhouses were also home to wasps, hornets, spiders, and other creatures. The general rule was, if you leave them alone, they'd leave you alone. Most of the time, that was the case.

My less-than-scientific survey of Facebook friends revealed that some of them had had access to "two-holers," with one even claiming to have seen a "four-holer."

I cannot for the life of me understand why anyone would want to share this experience with up to three people, but I will point out that still today, it is not uncommon to be eating in a restaurant and have a woman excuse herself to the restroom, and see three other women grab their purses and say, "We'll go with you."

The men remain at the table puzzled, but we are smart enough not to ask or want to know why they do that.

For those who have never been lucky enough to use an outhouse, you should try it if the opportunity presents itself. If for no other reason than to give you yet another reason to forever appreciate modern conveniences.

Those of us who have had the outhouse experience are dwindling in numbers. However, we readily share our experience and wear it as a badge of honor.

So, the next time you have a moment to appreciate the modern plumbing most of us now take for granted, take a second to thank Mr. Whipple. And go ahead and squeeze the Charmin.

Child's Play

There was a simple toy I used to love. It featured a bald man with big eyes and a red nose, who was shielded behind a plastic case. There was a red-handled wand, as it was called on the package, with a magnet on one end.

Inside the plastic case were metal shavings. If I placed the toy flat, I could use the magnetic wand to drag the shavings over the man's face, giving him hair on his head, a mustache, beard, or even hairy ears if I wanted.

The toy, which debuted in the mid-'50s, is called, "Wooly Willy," and like many of the toys of youth, you can still buy it today.

What made me think of this was a new toy that, according to Fortune Magazine, recently accounted for 17 percent of all online toy sales: The Fidget Spinner.

By the time I became aware that the Fidget Spinner (a triangular-shaped device you hold and spin between your finger and thumbs) was all the rage, I was told by some younger people that I'd missed the peak of its popularity. No matter. This wasn't the first fad toy that passed me by.

There have been a number of toys that have been quite popular. But, often, they vanished as quickly as they arrived. The frenzy that they created seems silly and even somewhat baffling in hindsight.

I can't speak to most toy fads of the last 20 years, but I can address the ones of my kids' childhoods.

The Rubik's Cube is a great example. A square of smaller, movable squares of different colors, the Rubik's Cube was actually a puzzle. Unlike a jigsaw puzzle, where it came unassembled and your job was to put it together, the cube came with all of the colors in the correct places, and you had to mess it up yourself and then try and fix it.

In the 1980s, stores sold out of the thing and people would line up on shipment day to get one. My kids and their friends would have contests to see who could fix theirs the quickest.

I still have one in a drawer somewhere that has a dent in it where it may have been accidentally thrown across the room.

Cabbage Patch Dolls were also a huge toy fad. I didn't understand them then and I still don't, but they were the must-have toy for a couple of Christmases.

Supposedly, these babies were born in said cabbage patch, then boxed up, complete with a birth certificate, shipped to a store and then sold. I always found that whole concept creepy, but that didn't stop millions of moms from wrestling in the aisles of stores across America over one of these dolls to make sure that their kid had one come Christmas morning.

Ho, Ho, Ho.

My generation had its own share of fad toys. In middle school, we had a toy we called "Click Clacks," but their actual name was "Clackers." Clackers had a metal ring connected to two pieces of heavy twine.

At the end of each piece of twine was a hard ball. I'm not sure what the ball was made of, but it was quite hard. The object of the toy was to swing the balls up and down so that they smacked each other in mid-air. My father said that the true object of the toy was to send kids to the emergency room.

Mood rings were also quite popular when I was young. When you put the ring on, the stone in it allegedly turned the color that matched the mood you were in at that moment. The ring came with a card that listed all of the colors and the moods they represented. Mine stayed black a lot. I'm guessing that since most teens are in a perpetually foul mood, the rings really did work.

The standout fad toy of my childhood to me was The Pet Rock. I never owned one, but lots of friends did. Kudos to the guy who came up with the idea to take a box, poke air holes in it, label it, "Pet Rock," and actually find people dumb enough to give him money for it. I hope he got really, really rich for pulling that one off.

It is worth noting that it's the basic toys and games that have retained their popularity with multiple generations: Lincoln Logs, Play-Doh, Silly Putty, Battleship, Monopoly, View-Master, the Hula Hoop and others have stood the test of time and are still available for kids and adults alike.

Now, if they can just come up with an updated Wooly Willy that puts real hair on the balding guys who played with that toy during their youth, they'll have another hit.

Life Lines

"Life is what happens while you are busy making other plans." – John Lennon, "Beautiful Boy" 1980

I don't mind birthdays. As a matter of fact, having them is quite preferable to not having them. It's just that most folks, regardless of our age, never feel old. We may be old, look old, and act old, but inside, we don't think of ourselves as aged.

In my head, I'm still a 16-year-old with my whole life ahead of me. On my driver license, I qualify for a discount at Denny's.

I attended a surprise birthday party for a friend. He turned 89.

I am punctual by nature, but more often than not, I'm early. Arriving almost 45 minutes ahead of the guest of honor, I was quite shocked to see that the venue where the party was held was already full. There were far more people than there were chairs in which to put them.

I decided to grab a glass of water and mingle, introducing myself to the others. I knew the birthday boy and his immediate family, but that was about it.

As I talked with most who were there, I discovered that some were family, but many were like me – friends that he's made during his almost nine decades. What struck me was the

36

wide age range of those attending and the distance that some had traveled to be there.

Some attendees had made a short drive to get there from other cities within Texas, or from towns in Arkansas, but others had come from much greater distances, including one man who had traveled all the way from India.

I couldn't help but wonder if, by God's will and grace, I live to be 89, would that many people make the effort just to wish me a happy birthday?

To me, the number of people at his birthday celebration was an indication of the kind of life this gentleman has lived and evidence that he made time for all of these individuals so that they felt that they mattered to him.

As I looked around the room, I wondered how many times in how many different ways he had positively impacted each of their lives.

Maybe it had been meals shared at holidays or possibly, he had stepped in at a time when they needed someone to fill a void. Regardless, the joy on the faces of everyone in attendance represented an obvious love, respect, and appreciation for him, and him for each of them.

Attending this special celebration made me take stock of my own life. My next birthday is just days after his and seeing how special he was to so many made me wonder whether I had utilized every opportunity that I've been given to make my life matter.

Often, many of us waste far too much time trying to get to the next thing on our checklist of things to do instead of savoring what's right in front of us. Some refer to it as stopping to smell the roses, but I prefer to call it, stopping to make people feel as if they matter.

A different friend of mine recently lost their job. After over three decades in the same field, they went to work one day, only to be told that they could go home. Their services were no longer needed.

This individual has done much for many over their career. It's hard to know what to say when someone shares with you that something like this just happened to them.

I reminded them that it's called "life," not because of any particular piece of it, but because of its entirety. Our time here isn't defined by any window of our existence, but by how we use every chapter. The best part of any new chapter is that we get to write it ourselves.

Like my birthday friend, it was each chapter that he had written that told the whole story in one room, on one day, with those whose lives he had touched.

As I watched the joy in the face of my 89-year-old friend while he hugged, laughed, and joked with those who came to his surprise birthday party, I committed to myself that whatever time that I have left, I will try my best to make it about others.

I believe that God gives each of us not just one but many purposes while we are here on earth. Some are obvious, while others may happen and we are none the wiser. But, I believe that focusing on others is the true key to happiness.

Because, a life well lived is one that is spent making others feel that they truly matter.

The Fouke Monster

When I was a kid in the early 1970s, the Fouke Monster was around every corner. At least, that was how I saw things as a 10-year-old.

For those who aren't familiar with this Sasquatch-like creature, the Fouke Monster allegedly roamed (some say, still roams) the river bottoms and woods in and around Fouke, Arkansas, which is about 40 miles southeast of where I grew up in Ashdown.

At the time, several newspapers were reporting about people who had not only seen a hairy, 7-foot-tall creature in and around the corner of Southwest Arkansas that borders Louisiana, but one family also claimed that the monster had reached through a window screen in their house and tried to get them.

Between the monsters that I was certain lived under my bed, and the Fouke Monster potentially putting his large, hairy hand and arm through my window, suffice it to say, my sleep was filled with less-than-pleasant dreams.

Many places in the country, and in other parts of the world for that matter, have local legends of monsters. New Jersey has the Jersey Devil, which witnesses describe as a horse-like creature with wings. Maine has Cassie, the giant sea serpent. West Virginia has the Mothman. And Arizona claims to have giant flying creatures called Thunderbirds, which have oral legends dating back to Native Americans in that area.

The Fouke Monster, also called the Boggy Creek Monster and Southern Sasquatch, according to some sources, has reported sightings going back to the mid-1800s. But most of the reports of the beast can be traced back to the 1940s.

Rumors of the monster came to a head for me and my classmates in 1972 when there were rumblings on the playground that someone was making a movie about the Fouke Monster.

What was circulating around the swing sets and monkey bars was that the movie would recreate many of the alleged sightings and that we would actually see what the monster looked like.

Well, heck. We were all in.

Even though everyone in my fifth-grade class was terrified of the Fouke Monster, but wouldn't admit it, we all had our fifty cents ready in our pants pocket to plunk down at the ticket window at Williams Movie Theater to see the film. We just had to wait patiently for the movie to finish production and come to town.

When *The Legend of Boggy Creek* finally hit movie theaters, it surprised a lot of people, but especially people in the film industry.

41

According to its Wikipedia page, it has made $25 million on a $160,000 budget. I remember hearing that it held the record for many years as the most profitable independent film in U.S. history.

The movie was directed by a very interesting man from Texarkana named Charles B. Pierce. He is now deceased, but I had the occasion to meet him twice.

When I was in Cub Scouts, my troop attended a taping of the local kids' show, *The Laugh-A-Lot Club*, which Charles hosted on local NBC affiliate KTAL-TV as the persona of Mayor Chuckles. In the early '80s, he contacted me about doing some narration for a film he was working on at the time. During both encounters, he was quite cordial.

He obviously was also quite savvy. He knew how to turn a little bit of money into a lot of money.

That movie launched the Fouke Monster from local lore to national attention. Not surprisingly, after the movie came out, more and more people came forward to claim that they had evidence of the monster or that they had encountered it.

Local men put together hunting parties to head out and try and bring back the creature. There were even stories of people who were charged with filing false reports.

The legend of the Fouke Monster carried on for a number of years, mainly through the late 1970s, but those of us who lived in the area eventually moved on and our interest waned.

That didn't stop the Fouke Monster franchise, however. A book called, *The Best of Boggy Creek: The True Story of the Fouke Monster* was published. And four other movies were also released: *Return to Boggy Creek; Boggy Creek II: And The Legend Continues; Boggy Creek: The Legend is True; and The Legacy of Boggy Creek.*

Obviously, interest in making a buck on the legend has lasted decades, as the last two movies mentioned were released in 2010 and 2011.

Even though reports of the Fouke Monster aren't picked up in the media much these days, the sightings have continued through the years, according to the monster's unofficial website, foukemonster.net. It lists sightings dating back to 1908, with the most recent from May of 2017.

It says: "A man and wife were driving south on I-49 near Boggy Creek at around dusk. As the woman looked toward the northbound lane, she saw a 'real tall, hairy human-like figure' standing at the tree line. She became terrified as she looked closer at the huge figure and exclaimed, 'What is that!?' Her husband was driving and could not look back fast enough to see the figure. The woman does not think it was a person."

I personally have never seen the Fouke Monster and I am a lot less worried about him these days than when I was 10. But, for those of us who grew up in the early '70s in Southwest Arkansas, he will forever be part of our childhood.

The Legend of Boggy Creek is available on DVD, but watch it at your own risk. And be sure to check under your bed before you turn in for the night.

Driving Without A License

I was sitting in the living room on the avocado green couch watching daytime TV when I heard the back door open.

I was the only one home, but I didn't even turn around to see who it was. In the mid-1970s in Arkansas, you didn't worry about who was coming in your house. People just let themselves in. Especially if it was a relative.

I heard my uncle's voice.

"Hey," he said. "I need you to drive a car home for me that I just bought."

"Yes, sir," I said. "Let me get my shoes on."

I started to put on my boots, but decided that my tennis shoes would likely be a better choice. I wanted to make sure that I had complete control of the brake and gas pedals. Particularly since I'd never actually driven a car before.

I was about 12 or 13 years old at the time. I'd driven several motorcycles, riding lawnmowers, and, at the request of my mother, had even backed the car out of the carport during the winter months to crank the engine and get the heater going.

Cranking the car in the winter was a good deal for both my mother and me. She got to slide into a toasty warm car when she took my sister and me to school, and I got to tell my buddies that I got to start the car that morning.

Today, you go out and turn on the key and the vehicle fires right up, runs smoothly, and can be driven almost immediately. But, 50 years ago, cars had to be caressed a bit to get them started and warmed up. Before you could head down the road, you had to pump the gas pedal (not too much or you'd flood the engine), turn the ignition, and then keep your foot on the gas just enough so that the car wouldn't die.

You always knew when you'd hit that sweet spot where the automatic choke was taking over. The engine would then smooth out. Once the engine was hot, so was the air coming out of the heater under the dash.

My mom letting me start the car for her from the time I was about nine or so allowed me to bluff my way through driving my uncle's newly acquired car.

Should I have told him that I'd never actually driven before? Sure, I should have. Was I going to? Not on your life.

I got into his truck and we headed over to a man's house. The car he bought was only a few years old at the time and I can still see it clearly in my mind. It was a 1971 Chevrolet Monte Carlo. It was pretty.

It was a typical color for the day. The car was gold, and if memory serves, it had a black vinyl top.

My uncle shook the man's hand, took the keys from him, and then handed them to me.

"Follow me home," he said.

"Yes, sir," I answered.

Reality began to set in. Should I come clean and tell him that I don't really know how to drive?

Nah.

I began to comb through my young mind, trying to recall watching my parents and other relatives drive so that I could do the best job possible.

Also, I fleetingly thought about how I'd seen Steve McQueen drive, but decided that I'd better stick to how I'd seen my mom drive and hold the Steve McQueen technique for another day.

I cranked the Monte Carlo after pumping the gas pedal a few times, held the pedal in just slightly after the engine cranked, and once the engine smoothed out, I put it in drive and pressed the accelerator.

The car lurched forward a little too much, so I backed off. With my hands at 10 and 2 on the steering wheel, I eased onto the roadway behind my uncle.

At this time, Ashdown, Arkansas, had just one blinking red light at the main intersection. There were no traffic lights with red, yellow and green. So, I watched how my uncle proceeded through stop signs, the blinking red light, and just did what he did.

Along the way, I weaved a little, but for the most part, I think I did just fine.

Obviously, my uncle didn't think I did too badly, either. He never said a word about my driving after we got to his house.

"Park it over there," he said when we arrived. So, I did.

I got out of the Monte Carlo and back into his truck.

He took me back home and left.

Thirty-plus years went by. At a family gathering, someone mentioned the old Monte Carlo and how much my uncle had loved that car. By this time, the car was long gone, having been wrecked by my cousin.

I decided it was now safe to come clean.

"You remember when he had me drive that car home when he bought it?" I asked my aunt.

"No, not really," she said.

"Well," I said. "The truth is, when he came by to get me that day, I'd never driven before."

"What?" she said.

"Yeah, I don't know how old he thought I was," I said. "But, I not only wasn't old enough to drive and didn't have a driver's license, I'd never driven a car."

She laughed.

I was glad she laughed. Even when you've reached my age you still have that feeling when you're around your parents, aunts and uncles that you might be on the verge of getting grounded.

Honesty is the best policy. But, I didn't lie that day about not knowing how to drive. I just wasn't asked the question.

Ms. Bobby

The building looked bigger, but I was certain it was the same one.

The last time I had been inside was 1977. I was 15, a sophomore in high school, and the facility's chief dishwasher. As a matter of fact, I'm fairly certain that I was the facility's only dishwasher.

County Seat Fried Chicken was my hometown's only fried chicken restaurant at the time. With a population of only slightly over 5,000 on the city limit sign, KFC and Church's didn't have franchises in towns as small as Ashdown back then.

Heck, we were lucky to have a Sonic.

But, being locally owned was in my favor. My mom and dad played cards with the wife of the guy who owned County Seat. So, it was fairly easy for me to get my first real job there. By "real," I mean a job where you clock in and out and pay taxes. Prior to that, I mowed yards.

Mr. Pete, the owner, hired me to do what most teens do at a restaurant. I cleaned.

In addition to washing dishes, I also swept, mopped, and maintained the fryers.

Now, let me tell you, running the fryers properly made less of a mess and made the dishwashing, sweeping, and mopping much easier. Ms. Bobby taught me that.

I never knew Ms. Bobby's last name. I never asked. One name was all she needed. Everyone just knew her as that.

She was happy, loud, wise, and an excellent cook. If she liked you, she would share her happiness and wisdom with you. Fortunately, she liked me.

I'm guessing that Ms. Bobby was in her 50s at the time. She loved to sing while she cooked. One day shortly after I started, I was trying to slide the drain bucket underneath the chicken fryer, when her singing stopped. She'd been watching me without me knowing it.

"Young man," she said. "You need to tilt that there bucket before you turn on that drain. Let the oil even out in the bottom of the bucket and

51

then as it fills, sit the bucket flat on the floor. That way, it won't fall over and make a mess you ain't gonna be wantin' to clean."

"Yes, ma'am. Thank you," I said.

She looked at me to make sure I was actually listening and not just giving her lip service. When I followed her directions, she smiled at me and resumed her singing.

In the days, weeks, and months that followed, Ms. Bobby took me under her wing. In between me washing dishes, sweeping, mopping, and keeping the oil fresh in the fryers, she taught me how to quickly, but effectively, peel a potato.

She also taught me how to mash potatoes at the right temperature while adding the correct amount of butter, milk, salt, and pepper. It's the recipe I use to this day.

She showed me how to dip the chicken pieces in an egg and milk mix before coating it in flour. It was a process you repeated twice more before gently sliding the chicken into the hot peanut oil near the front edge of the fryer. This technique helped keep splashing oil off of the floor. She was showing me how to be efficient, which kept the sweeping and mopping to a minimum.

Ms. Bobby mixed the shredded cabbage and carrots together and then added the mayo and spices to make coleslaw. So simple, yet delicious.

But, it was her peach cobbler that kept the place in business.

She would roll the dough over and over before putting it in place. The fresh peaches, sugar, milk, cinnamon and other ingredients were all mixed to perfection and then poured into place in the long, stainless steel pans. As the large oven baked Ms. Bobby's cobbler, the whole place began to smell like Heaven.

I worked there for a little over a year before taking a new job sacking groceries at the Piggly Wiggly. I thanked Mr. Pete for the opportunity and gave Ms. Bobby a goodbye hug.

"You remember all I showed you," she said. "You can cook it yourself. If you just remember."

I never saw her again.

Over the last four decades, I thought of Ms. Bobby every now and then when I made mashed potatoes or ate peach cobbler. But on this recent day, the vividness of her presence was front and center.

As my wife and I entered the building, I said, "This is the same place, I'm sure of it."

Little was left of the original layout, but the ceiling, with its shiplap-style wood, was unmistakable.

County Seat Fried Chicken is no longer there. The original restaurant and Bobby are both long gone. The building had housed a bank for several years, then a pawn shop, but it's now a restaurant again. They specialize in desserts.

On this day, I was the guest speaker at the meeting of the local book club. My book was being featured. Instead of changing the oil in the fryers in the kitchen, I was a guest in the dining room.

Leading the book club was my English teacher from my senior year, Mrs. Martha Trusley. Two years after I had hugged Ms. Bobby goodbye, Mrs. Trusley kept me after class one day to tell me that I had a gift for writing and should pursue it.

Things had come full circle. I just wish that Ms. Bobby had been there to see it.

CHAPTER THREE – FAMILY ALBUM

I Love You, Too

You can always tell from the timbre of the voice of the person on the other end of the line when bad news is coming.

A thousand things go through your mind during the milliseconds between the realization that what you're about to hear will change your life forever and receiving the rest of the message.

It was my father. He asked if I was sitting down.

My mother had just left a couple of hours earlier from a visit with my wife and was headed back to Arkansas. I assumed that he was about to tell me that there had been an accident.

There had been no accident. My mother was fine.

My sister was not. She had died of a heart attack.

She was only 52.

The bottom fell out of me.

The days that followed were a whirlwind of travel, notifying family and friends, making arrangements, and overwhelming grief.

Time seemed to move at light speed one minute and stand still the next. It was surreal.

As I tried to make sense of it all, two things emerged in my mind. One, she passed in her sleep, which was a blessing. Two, she was at a good place in life when she went.

There's never a good time to go, but she was at about as good of a place as you can be when she went to be with the Lord. She had a family who loved her, three grandchildren, and a job she found rewarding.

My sister was an outgoing person. But, she wasn't always that way.

As a child, she was scared of a lot of things. She was afraid of people she didn't know, afraid to have her picture taken, and she was terrified of Santa Claus.

There was just the two of us, and as her older brother it was my duty to advise her that being afraid of Santa and refusing to have your picture made with him was a great way to have Santa skip our house on Beech Street come Christmas morning.

I can remember riding in the back seat of our '60 model Buick Le Sabre on the way to Sears to see Santa and telling her that she needed to not cry or she was going to blow it for the both of us.

The photos of us with Santa show my sister with bloodshot eyes and me with an ear-to-ear grin. In spite of my warnings and her crying, Santa still came to see us.

But, as she got older she came out of her shell. She had lots of friends, made the cheerleading squad, and was one of the prettiest and most popular girls in her class.

She was smart. Good grades came easy to her. She was artistic. Her drawings and sketches won awards.

My buddies hung out at my house fairly often. We were a couple of years older, so we found my sister and her friends to be highly annoying. That is, until they were about 14 years old.

Suddenly, my sister's friends weren't so annoying. My buddies and I began to encourage them to visit the house more often.

I eventually graduated, left home, and started a family. So did my sister.

She worked in a number of different fields during her career, including the legal profession and in the restaurant business. But it was her final career field where she found her true calling: home health.

I honestly don't know how she wound up getting a job taking care of people in their homes, but it was obvious that she had a passion for it. The way she talked about each person she took care of sounded as if she was describing one of her own family members.

It takes a special person to do that type of job. Her hours were long (10-12 hour shifts), the work was hard, and often, those she helped were handicapped, had a disability, an end-of-life illness, or all of the above. But, her feelings for each of those she served were real.

It amazed me that this was the same person who, decades earlier, cried around people she didn't know.

My sister had a life like most. There were ups. There were downs. But, she always stayed positive. If there were obstacles in the road, she went around them. If there were fires, she put them out.

She loved to laugh. She loved to make other people laugh. My sister always enjoyed a good joke and tried to have a new one for you when she saw you or talked to you.

And she always ended our conversations with, "I love you."

But, I wasn't the only one to whom she said that. She ended all of the conversations with those she cared about with, "I love you." Goodnight, Renee'. I love you, too.

Father Time

My earliest memories of my dad are of his smiling face and his laugh.

And his singing. As he would hold me tightly and pat my back, the resonance of his baritone voice in my ears and against my chest gave me what every child needs – attention and the assurance of unquestionable love.

I believe that he sang to me, and later to my younger sister, for many reasons. He enjoyed singing, but I also believe that singing was how he connected with us.

When we were young, my sister and I shared a room. At bedtime, we had our routine. Baths, brush our teeth, climb onto our beds, and then call for him. Our dad would then stand in the darkened doorway and softly begin our goodnight song.

Peter, Paul and Mary's, "Puff The Magic Dragon," filled our room as we faded into a deep, comforted sleep.

In the early 1960s, many fathers were distant. Raising the kids was left to the moms. I don't think that this parenting approach was intentional. It was just what dads had learned from their fathers. It was a holdover from a generation that viewed men who showed affection as weak.

My father didn't care what anyone thought. Public displays of affection for me and my sister were the norm. He never had a problem with giving hugs or a kiss, anywhere and in front of anyone. He was proud that he loved his children and he wanted the world to know it.

I can't emphasize enough how unique that was for the time. But I never gave it a second thought.

In middle school and junior high, he would sometimes take me to school and pick me up. As we arrived in his 1964 Ford Falcon, he always said, "I love you, son," as I lifted my book satchel from the floorboard and got out to go to my first class of the day.

I can't honestly say that I was proud to be exiting a 1964, four-door Ford Falcon while the other kids were getting out of new Ford LTDs, Chevy Impalas, and Cadillacs (to my dad, cars weren't for looks, they were for transportation), but I can say that I was probably one of the few boys whose dads were not only dropping them off at school, but were also hearing, "I love you."

My dad was switched to a night shift when I was about 12. He didn't like it and neither did we; but like most hard-working folks, he accepted it and did the best he could.

He's always credited my mom with raising us, since she was home with us the most and managed all of our activities (guitar lessons and sports for me, and twirling for my sister, and art lessons for us both) while she also worked a job.

61

But his commitment to doing whatever it took to make sure that he kept a good job so that we had a nice roof over our heads, something to eat, clothes, and school supplies, was a lesson for me. One that I embraced later in life when I was raising two sons.

Like a lot of kids, sleepovers were an inexpensive weekend activity that my buddies and I enjoyed. We would take turns spending the night at each other's houses.

One weekend, I had spent the night with my best friend, Jeff, who lived in Alleene, Arkansas, which is out in the country. When my dad rolled up in the driveway early the next morning to pick me up he was driving his 1966 white Ford Mustang.

He had substantially upgraded from the Falcon.

After my dad and I left and got to the crossroads to turn and head to Ashdown, he pulled over and stopped on the side of the road.

I asked what was wrong.

"Nothing," he said. "It's time you learned how to drive."

Back then, kids learned early how to drive everything from cars, to trucks, to tractors. We changed seats and he explained to me how the clutch and accelerator worked in combination, and how to shift gears. Off we went.

He later showed me how to work on the car – how to change the oil, bleed the brakes, change the points and condenser, change a flat, and rotate the tires.

When I was 16, he gave me the Mustang.

As I made my way through high school, I counted on him for advice for everything from whether to take shop class to how to understand girls (he told me to take shop class, but that I was on my own on the last one).

My dad has always been there for me. Whether he was praising me or correcting me, he was firm, but loving.

I learned how to be a dad from him.

My children will tell you that while they were growing up, I would sing to them as I tucked them in. I picked them up from sleepovers, taught them how to drive, showed them how to work on cars, but left them to their own understanding of the fairer sex.

They might not have been proud to have been picked up in a 1971 Oldsmobile Cutlass Sport Coupe while the other kids were getting into new Ford LTDs, Chevy Impalas, and Cadillacs (cars weren't for looks, they were for transportation), but they always heard, "I love you," when they got in the car.

I grew up thinking that everyone had a great dad, but later learned that that isn't always the case. Thankfully, it was for my sister and me. The love and pride he expresses has been a constant.

That's why we have Father's Day. For dads like mine.

A Lure of Life

I don't remember much about it, but I do remember riding a train.

The adventure began with a discussion about passenger train rides coming to an end. My mom and grandmother were discussing how sad it was that, before long, you wouldn't be able to use the train as a means of travel.

The decision was made to take me on a train
ride before the opportunity was gone.

I was about three years old.

This memory came back to me as we were
going through my father's things. My mom
relayed something my father had said to her
after my sister passed away.

"Life is like a train. Some get on. Some get off,"
he told her. He wasn't being flippant. That's just
how my dad was. He was trying to comfort her.

Just shy of a year later, my sister was there to
greet him when he also got off the train.

During a time when most families are planning
their Thanksgiving menu, we were sorting
through a lifetime of acquired possessions.
Getting ready for an estate sale.

I would build up a good pace of sorting and
stacking items, then would be stopped in my
tracks by an item that brought back a specific
memory.

My father enjoyed many things, but fishing was
a special passion of his. I wish that I could say
that I inherited his love of being an angler, but I

didn't. But, he did take me fishing enough when I was a kid that I remembered certain favorite fishing gear that he had.

Some fishermen like fancy rods and reels and expensive lures, but not my dad. His tastes in fishing equipment were basic. He liked the Zebco 33 reel and simple baits.

And I found a lot of both. As a matter of fact, I stopped counting the Zebco reels. There were buckets full of them. I was astonished at how many there were.

I guess he didn't want to run out.

I can recall being in a boat with him and being shown how to tie a lure. It was a wooden lure, painted red and white, with silver spinners on the sides. He would cast it into the water and slowly reel it in.

I don't recall whether he caught anything with that lure while I was with him that day, but I saw it again in his tackle box on numerous other occasions.

But that was half a century ago, and most fishing lures don't make it very long. They get caught up in underwater brush or in a tree limb and are cut loose and left.

I hadn't thought about that lure in decades, but as I opened one of his many tackle boxes, there it was. It was now yellowed, and the paint had faded, but I recognized it immediately.

It was much smaller than I remembered. Fitting inside one of the inset compartments in the top tray, one of the eyes stared back at me as I looked at it and marveled that it was still around.

I closed the tackle box and placed it in my truck. I'm not a fisherman, but this was going home with me. I couldn't part with it.

There were many other items that brought back memories, but I tried to keep going to stay focused. We had a lot to go through and much to do.

But, it seemed that every other item brought back a slice of another time in life. A time that only remained in my mind, but remained, nonetheless.

Almost eight decades of things were now being sorted and stacked. Soon, they would belong to someone else.

My father loved estate sales. I'm sure that together, we went to hundreds of them. It was a chance to find something useful at a good price. The items that had once brought pleasure to the previous owner, we would now use.

One in particular came back to me. My father, mother, and I stopped at one in Texas. It was at least 20 years ago. My mom was in another part of the residence and my dad and I were together. We walked into a room and there, on the floor, was a name tag. I picked it up and examined it. It was a work badge.

Dad and I discussed how this was the person's identity. It was who they were. It represented how they made their living, where they went every day. And now, they were gone, and people they never met were going through their things.

Us. We were the people they never met who were going through their things.

But, my dad reminded me that they were just things. Things that had served the person while they were on the earth, and that likely, that person would be glad that someone else would find the same value that they had placed in them.

I put the badge on a shelf, and we went on with our shopping.

And now, it was time for others to find usefulness in my father's things. As I thought back to the discussion, he and I had about the name badge, I became OK with what I was having to do with my dad's possessions.

At the end of a long, hard and physical day, we finally sat down and began to rest. That's when my mom told me what my dad had said about life being like a train.

I thought about my sister, my dad, and the train ride.

I got up, went to my truck, and opened the tackle box to take another look at the old, wooden lure. I closed it and headed for the shower to wash the tired off of myself.

As I said, I don't fish, but while cleaning up, I decided to start. I want to see why fishing brought such pleasure to my father.

It's something I want to do before I get off the train.

Are We There Yet?

Lying on the deck behind the backseat and
staring upward through the rear glass of a Buick
gave a kid the perfect view of the sky and
clouds.

A cloud could look like a bear one moment and
a crocodile the next.

Family road trips of the 1960s and 70s
obviously did not have safety at the forefront,
but boy, were the car rides memorable.

No family I knew had enough money to ride in
airplanes to their destination. So, we, and all of
our relatives and friends, took the family car to
Carlsbad Caverns, Dodge City, Kansas, Disney
World, or wherever else our brood was going
that year.

Deck sailing (what I called lying behind the
backseat) was just one of a handful of options
available to a child to pass the time on a family
summer vacation.

Others included standing on the hump behind
the front seat and peering between your parents,
through the windshield, and over the long white
hood of the 1960 Le Sabre; reading comic

books, drawing, or showing your artistic prowess on an Etch A Sketch.

Fifty years ago, cars were built to comfortably accommodate large families. You could easily put a family of six in the average sedan and still have room leftover inside for a Volkswagen Beetle.

On the longest road trips, sitting in the backseat and staring out the window was the least exciting option. My dad would tell my sister and me to "count the cows," but that lost its luster faster than just about anything else on a long drive.

After you had exhausted all of the other possibilities, there was always the enjoyable leg of the trip spent trying to defend yourself to your parents when your sibling screamed, "He touched me!" "He's messing with me!" or "He's looking at me!"

My family never owned a station wagon, but my grandmother and some of my friends' families did. I always thought that station wagons were the perfect vehicle for taking trips. You could put four to eight adults in the front and back seat, and then stack children on top of each other in the back by the swing outdoor.

The nicer station wagons had a big, electric window in the back door. Most people today would be mortified to have witnessed this, but it was quite common to see a Ford Country Squire barreling down a two-lane highway with six kids hanging out of the open, back window.

Flailing our arms and waving at everyone we passed was another way to occupy ourselves as we continued on to our destination.

Reading barn roofs was another way to pass the time. "Visit Jesse James Hideout – Meramec Caverns, U.S. 66, Stanton, Mo." was painted on the tops of many a farmer's barn as a means of advertising a tourist stop. It was not uncommon to see dozens of them. Today, spotting one is a rare treat.

Singing was also a trip option for kids in a car. "Puff the Magic Dragon" was the one most often kicked off by my father as he steered and tried to engage us. As we got older, sometimes the sing-along songs were current hits that emanated from the AM radio in the dash, and its two speakers; one in the dash and the other in the back deck where we would take turns deck sailing.

Coloring books were another opportunity to fend off road trip boredom. On one particular trip, my parents gave me a "Jungle Book" traceable edition. In between each page of images of Mowgli and Baloo, there were pieces of onionskin paper. This allowed me to trace the images with a pencil before I colored the paper pages with my 64-count box of Crayola Crayons.

Riding down the road, I would go through some colors faster than others. Green went rapidly because of coloring the grass, and blue went fast from coloring the sky. I would peel back the paper from each crayon and sharpen it in the back of the Crayola box, then continue on.

You just had to remember not to leave your crayons in the car, lest 64 colors became one melted blob.

Each activity would always be interspersed with, "Are we there, yet?"

Kids now have iPods, cell phones, and other isolating distractions for when they travel. That's all well and good, but I'd never trade any of those for the memories of singing "Puff the Magic Dragon" with my dad.

Old Man's Winter

During one of global warming's many vacations where I live, record-low temps were set and kids and grown-ups got a few days off from school and work.

My wife and I have lived in an empty nest for a number of years now, but it was fun seeing pictures and video of our grandchildren on the east coast sliding on their sleds from the top to the bottom of the hill in their front yard, and then trek back up to repeat until they wore their mother out.

Also, the news and social media were filled with images and video of parents and children spending time together frolicking in the snow and ice. Makeshift sleds, from trashcan lids to flattened cardboard boxes, allowed kids, moms and dads to giggle and make memories together. My personal favorite was the video of the kids, they might have been 3 or 4, using a plastic laundry basket as their snowmobile.

There's something about snow, especially for those of us who've only known 20-minute Southern winters all of our lives that changes us. And it changes us for the better.

Snow days allow us to stop the world that controls us and, if only for a few days, gives us control of our time. Time to spend not punching a clock or studying a textbook, but time with each other.

What always amazes me is how, when Mother Nature freezes us in, we revert to things we did during the ice and snowstorms of our childhoods. Things that our parents learned from their childhoods, and their parents from theirs.

My sister and I would press our noses against the big living room windows.

"Momma! It's snowing! Can we make snow ice cream?"

Smiling, she would nod.

We'd bundle up and put on our gloves, then each grab a big bowl and head outside.

Mom would guide us on how to take the snow off of the trunk of the Buick. The trick was to get the top layer. It was the clean snow.

With bowls full, we would head to the kitchen where mom would mix in sugar, Pet Milk, and vanilla.

We'd peel off our coats and gloves and sit down in front of the console TV with a big spoon.

Savoring every scoop, we'd scrape the bottom of the bowl as we watched "Bewitched" or one of our other favorites.

We would go out into our front yard and try to build a snowman, but he never was a very large snowman since we were lucky to get a couple of inches of snow. But, he was still our snowman and we'd proudly call our mom and dad outside to tell us how good we had done.

When I was 15, we had three weeks of significant winter weather. Every Wednesday for 21 days, there was some form of winter precipitation. The first Wednesday, it rained and then froze. The second Wednesday, it sleeted and snowed. The third, it snowed some more.

My best friend Clint and I bundled up and made our way through an empty lot to a construction site. There we found large piles of dirt, which to us had turned into slopes like the finest ski resort in Aspen.

We uncovered some flattened cardboard boxes, dusted the ice and snow off of them, and spent the next several hours shoving each other down those hills.

When we finally called it quits, I think that's the coldest I'd ever been. I had no feeling in my feet, and my hands barely worked. I wish I could go back and do it again.

Heading home, we peeled off our boots and soaked socks and stuck our feet and then our hands in front of the fireplace. The rest of the day was spent with warm drinks, jigsaw puzzles, and playing canasta.

My kids loved playing in winter weather. Shortly after we moved to Texas in the late '80s, it iced and snowed one Christmas Eve. We lost electricity, but between family quilts, an old Aladdin Lamp, and a charcoal grill, we did fine. An ice storm in the early 2000s left the entire city without electricity. The first question our then-teenage son asked was, "How are we going to eat?"

Since his diet consisted solely of Hot Pockets and microwave ovens, he was quite concerned about the possibility of starvation.

He marveled that you could wrap Hot Pockets in aluminum foil and place them in a cake pan in the gas fireplace. We all ate Hot Pockets and watched Wheel of Fortune on his small, battery-operated handheld TV.

It's one of my favorite memories.

We've allowed our worlds to spin faster. So fast that we don't spend the time with each other that we should.

So maybe, just maybe, these little winter respites arrive for a reason. To give us the moments we should already be taking to stop what we're doing, spend time with each other, and laugh, love, and reflect.

Because it's the snow ice cream, snowmen, and sledding that build the warmest memories.

CHAPTER FOUR – IT'S THE HOLIDAY SEASON

Christmas Present

Rising quietly from the bed as not to wake her, I dress in the dark and make my way to the door. I open it and walk into the hallway. On the bedroom wall, I watch the dim light shining in from the living room narrow and then disappear as I lightly close the door.

As I make the short walk from our bedroom to the living room, the light brightens. It's 3 o'clock on Christmas morning and the lights on the tree have been on all night. I walk over to it and stare.

Angels. There are lots of angels. Many are glass and hand-blown. They are fragile and beautiful. Some are gifts from her family, others she acquired herself.

I stare at the bubble lights. Shaped like a candle that sits in a holder, the bubble lights still mesmerize me as much as they did five decades ago when I was a child. Tiny bubbles shoot toward the top of the glass cylinder from what seems to be an endless supply.

For a moment in my mind, I'm once again five years old, standing in footed pajamas and looking at the cedar my father hand-cut in the forest and brought home in the back of his 1952 Chevrolet truck. The tree is covered with lights, but also with handmade decorations that I crafted in Sunday School.

Back in the moment, my eyes move to the red ribbons, which are carefully tied to the tree limbs. Their concave reflection in the golden round ornaments accentuates the intricate and unique patterns of each ribbon.

I turn and head for the kitchen and plug in the percolator. As it begins to make the sound that only a 60-year-old percolator does, I put on my heavy coat, gloves, and hat, and exit the back door. Loading my arms with as much firewood as I can carry, I reenter the house and carefully stack each piece on the hearth. The embers from the Christmas Eve fire are enough to easily reignite a new blaze.

I carefully load each piece of wood into the stove, close and latch the door, and watch through the glass as the blaze begins to flicker and then roar.

In the kitchen, the light on the percolator glows. I pour a cup of black coffee and settle into my chair. The cat leaps into my lap, and we both take a moment: she to curl up and begin dozing, and me to reflect on all of my blessings.

I say a word of thanks for my wife, who still sleeps down the hall but will soon rise and round the corner into the living room with a smile on her face and a greeting of "Good morning, honey." Just as she always does.

I say thanks for the blessings that are our children, grandchildren, and our extended families. Thanks for a warm home, for food in the pantry, for neighbors who are also friends, and for our health.

The cat gladly takes over my chair as I rise to stoke the fire and get another cup of coffee. I return to the living room and stare at the lights on the tree. I look at the bubbles flowing rapidly inside each light, and I think about how many Christmases have passed in my lifetime.

It is easy to allow the Christmas season to pass without spending time focusing on why we celebrate it.

The quiet of the early hours each Christmas morning is the perfect opportunity to reflect on each of our blessings and on the short window of time on earth that each of us have been given to enjoy them.

Making the most of each Christmas and sharing its meaning with others is the best way to make the season merry.

Time is fleeting, but the meaning of Christmas is eternal.

"For unto you is born this day in the city of David a Savior, which is Christ the Lord." – Luke 2:11.

All Strung Out

Thanksgiving weekend is a special one for husbands. We put up Christmas decorations under the direction of our wives.

There are many things no one tells you before you get married, but one of the best-kept secrets that women successfully hide from men is the mandatory hanging of the Christmas decorations.

While single men across the nation ring in the holiday season watching sports in their underwear, married men bundle up, put on their mountain-climbing gear and hang from the eaves of their homes to string lights, hook up blinking reindeer, and set up inflatable Santas on their front lawns.

I'm not sure which strand of the female DNA includes the decoration compulsion, but I know that most of them have it in their makeup. Like clockwork, Thanksgiving ends and women feel the uncontrollable urge to have their husbands climb into a dusty attic, drag down 23 boxes of decorations, unpack them and put them out on display.

I've never been to the North Pole, but I'd highly doubt that even Santa puts up that much stuff.

If it were up to men, we'd stack empty beer cans in the shape of a tree in the corner of the living room and spray it with that fake snow in a can.

My high school classmate Jeanenne told me that she has 36 Christmas trees in her 2,000-square-foot house in Little Rock. She also has an antique Ford truck covered in over 1,000 lights, and an 11-foot nutcracker who stays in one of her beds. I love my friend Jeanenne. Her dad was one of the barbers in my hometown and cut my hair growing up.

But, lest my wife get any additional decorating ideas, we won't be visiting her in Little Rock during the holiday season.

When I was a kid, we went out into the woods Thanksgiving weekend and cut a live tree.

It was always cold, and my father spent most of our excursion keeping my sister and me focused on the task at hand. After trudging through the forest and cutting down the selected cedar with a handsaw, we'd drag the tree back out, tie it to the top of the car, and off we'd go to set it up at home.

My mom would get the lights out and we'd cross our fingers that one of the bulbs hadn't gone out since the last Christmas. If one bulb was out, the whole string didn't work.

My sister and I would pop popcorn, string it with a needle and thread and then add it to the tree. We also had silver tinsel. Angels and other figures we'd made out of construction paper in school and Sunday School were put on the limbs.

To this day, whenever I smell a cedar tree, I think of Christmas in 1960s Arkansas.

I'm sure my father felt the same pressure to go all out with the Christmas decorations that I, and now my sons, feel.

It's a rite of passage, I guess.

So, as I sit here lacing up my mountain-climbing boots and checking the spikes on the bottom of both to ensure I don't fall off the roof, I salute those of you who never take your Christmas lights down.

The rest of the year, people make fun of you. But, right now, you look like the smartest person in the world.

Let's Put the Thanks Back In Thanksgiving

Most of us celebrate Thanksgiving without a second thought. That's not how it was intended.

Contrary to what many say, America was founded on religious principles. Thanksgiving is proof of that.

Those who fled England to come here in the early 1600s did so for religious reasons. The first recognized Thanksgiving was a feast they shared with Native Americans to honor the Creator.

Since 1863, by proclamation of President Abraham Lincoln, Thanksgiving has been celebrated as a federal holiday on the fourth Thursday of November. Lincoln said it would be a day of, "Thanksgiving and Praise to our beneficent Father who dwelleth in the Heavens."

I find it amusing that those who argue that we should take religion out of everything never blink an eye when they take off on Thanksgiving or Christmas Day. If you know of anyone who has a problem with those who believe in God, but they still insist on going to work on one of these holidays, I'd like to meet them and shake their hand for sticking to their beliefs.

Thanksgiving is unique. Its sole purpose is to say thank you to God.

It was not designated as a day of overeating and watching football. It was set aside as a day for all of us to stop what we're doing, think about everything for which we should be grateful, and tell Him thank you for it.

That's it.

But, how many of us actually still do that?

Public prayer and praying aloud at home used to be common. Now, the former is almost non-existent, and the latter I see far less than I used to. I highly suspect that our lack of prayer, and consequently our lack of appreciation for virtually everything, is one of the reasons that our country is full of people who expect everything to be given to them and have no gratitude when it is.

Giving thanks does a simple thing: It makes us cognizant of what we have and how very lucky we are to have it.

Those born since World War II, my generation included, were blessed with so much, so quickly and so easily, that we have known very little want. Many of us may not have had everything we wanted, but we certainly have had most of what we needed. Very few of us have any idea what it is like to truly be in need.

Sadly, our over abundance of blessings has ironically led to a holiday that focuses on gluttony and the gridiron, rather than God and gratitude.

We should be on our knees daily, not just on Thanksgiving. Prayer provides us a type of communication that our smart phones never will – a direct connection to God.

So, this Thanksgiving, let's put down our phones, turn off the TV, join hands, bow our heads, and give thanks.

Because, Lord knows we have a lot to be thankful for.

Happy Holidaze

The holidays all run together now. I don't mean literally, I mean at the store.

Used to be, when you went into a Ben Franklin 5 & 10, Western Auto, Otasco, or Sears, you knew what holiday it was.

If it was almost Halloween, the appropriate decorations, costumes, and candy were on the shelf. My mom would take my sister and me to the store and we'd pick out a costume and then patiently wait for October 31 to roll around so that we could dress up and go trick or treating.

Come November, the same was true for fall decorations and items. As my mom prepared for Thanksgiving, we'd head back to the same stores. The Halloween items were gone, save for the bags of candy that didn't sell and had been deeply discounted (mostly large quantities of candy corn, but rarely Snickers, M&Ms, or the other good stuff).

We'd see decorations such as autumn wreaths, horns of plenty, wicker baskets, and other items that could be placed in the house or outside your front door.

After Thanksgiving, the stores would then display Christmas items. Large, plastic Santas with a light bulb inside were always amazing to me. They were huge.

You could sit them on your front porch or somewhere else in front of your house and they looked so great to those who drove by. I always wanted a big, plastic light bulb Santa, but we never bought one. I'm guessing that they were expensive and we weren't the Clampetts, so we had other, smaller decorations.

The Christmas decoration we had that I remember the most were the electric candles my mom would put in the window. The stems were white plastic and the light bulbs were shaped like candle flames. My mom still has the electric candles and still puts them in the window every year. They have to be over 50 years old and they still come to life when she gets them out of storage, sets them on the sill, and plugs them in.

They just don't make things as good as they used to.

After Thanksgiving, when the candles were in their rightful place in the window, my dad would load us and a hand saw into the Buick and we'd head out to one of the rural areas near where we lived to find a cedar for our Christmas tree.

Store-bought trees were available back then, but they were expensive and not many people had them, that I can recall. The exception was the gosh-awful aluminum trees with the lighted color wheel.

My grandmother had one of the aluminum trees and I can't tell you how much I detested it. If there is such a thing as "Christmas Gawdy," the aluminum Christmas tree is it. It always looked like a hippy stoner had partaken and then designed the thing. It basically was a wooden shaft with wires coming out that were supposed to represent the limbs and leaves. The leaves were some sort of flimsy metal, possibly Reynolds Aluminum Foil.

I remember this garish "tree" being in my grandparents' living room next to the console stereo. The ceiling light would be turned off and the color wheel would turn and change the silver to green, blue and red. Doesn't that just scream Christmas?

I still find these trees loathsome, but somehow, they have become highly collectible. Look them up on eBay. People are paying ridiculous money for these things. For the life of me, I have no idea why.

But today, the lines between the holidays have been erased. You can't walk into a Walmart before the end of summer without seeing Christmas or fall items. Halloween costumes and bags of candy corn (that will later be available on clearance) now sit either side by side or on the same aisles.

I don't know about you, but I liked it the way it was in the old days. If it was Halloween time, you only saw Halloween items for sale. The same was true for Thanksgiving and Christmas.

If I were a kid these days, I'd be completely confused.

Of course, all of this boils down to selling as much merchandise as possible. It's not about the holidays or the seasons any longer. It's about the almighty dollar.

Maybe I'm just naive and it always was about the money, but at least when I was a kid it seemed as if the storeowners wanted it to look like Halloween at Halloween, and Christmas when it was Christmas.

There's just something not right about being able to walk though a store and throw both a Batman costume and a plastic light bulb Santa inside into your buggy.

It's all so confusing. So, just to make sure I'm doing this correctly, I plan on wearing a Batman mask while I place an autumn wreath on the door and order myself a plastic, light bulb Santa and some electric candles like my mom has.

Happy HalloweenThanksgivingChristmas, everyone.

Thanksgiving Monopoly

With the arrival of the holidays, many universal family rituals return. When individuals who haven't seen each other since last Thanksgiving (or sometimes even longer) reunite to partake of good food, football, and gossip about the relatives who didn't show up, inevitably, out come the board games, decks of cards, and puzzles.

Now, you're either all in or all out on games and puzzles at Thanksgiving and Christmas. Some people live for the annual eight-hour game of Monopoly. Others would rather eat three large Pyrex dishes of green bean casserole or the "Ring Around the Tuna" Jell-O recipe than endure a game, which is seldom played by the actual rules.

By the way, I'm not making that last one up about the Jell-O. It's a real recipe. It has chunks of tuna, pimientos, and cucumbers folded inside lime Jell-O. But, I'll save disgusting holiday recipes that no one likes, but never admits that they don't like, for another column.

Gathering around the dining room or a card table to play board games, work a puzzle, or play cards during the holidays is a tradition in my family and many others.

When I was a kid, the children in the family would drag out my grandmother's Monopoly game and set it up on a card table in the sitting room. The sitting room was the room that every person born between the late 1800s and 1925 had, that was filled with nice furniture that was covered in plastic. Even though the furniture had enough plastic to protect it from nuclear fallout, no one was ever allowed to sit on the couch or chairs.

Back to Monopoly. We would try to acquire nice property and lots of money without going to jail. That's a good goal in life, by the way, but again, I digress.

After a couple of hours of playing Monopoly without arguing, eventually one of the participants would disagree with someone else's interpretation of a rule and a parent would be summoned from their card game in the kitchen.

This normally ended with the two or three kids who were arguing being sent outside into the cold with instructions to play football or something else, and to not come back in the house until they could straighten up and fly right.

I still don't know what that means.

In the kitchen, pots of percolator coffee flowed freely. As the adults guzzled large quantities of Maxwell House and played bridge or spades, they would reminisce about those who were no longer with us, days gone by, or discuss how our country was on the fast track to Hades.

It's funny how people's perceptions of things don't change much, even decades later.

Other board games for the younger kids would include Candy Land, Chutes and Ladders, Operation, Trouble, Connect Four, and Battleship. I always liked Battleship, even when I was older.

My mom's mother loved jigsaw puzzles. Consequently, there were plenty of jigsaw puzzles available to strew across an extra card table and begin working on. Quite often, the photo on the lid of the puzzle box depicted a country church, a pastoral scene, or a picture of kittens or puppies.

We seldom ever finished a jigsaw puzzle, unless my grandmother was helping us. Like the game of dominoes, my grandmother had an uncanny ability to play and win at dominoes or quickly assemble a jigsaw puzzle, even if the puzzle had a lot of pieces.

As each of the kids got older, we would be invited to the adult tables. I'm not just referring to playing cards, I'm referring to eating meals. That's how you knew that you were no longer considered a kid. If you were invited to eat at a table that didn't have folding legs, you were now viewed as all grown up.

This Thanksgiving, my wife and I will spend time at both her family's and at mine. I expect there will be a game of spades or hearts, and quite possibly a jigsaw puzzle thrown into the mix.

Monopoly has been mothballed at holiday gatherings the last few years, so I'm not expecting to have to hope for a good roll of the dice and enough money to acquire Park Place and Boardwalk.

But I am praying that the food selection does not include any tuna-infused Jell-O.

And, if one of the kids brings Battleship, I'm definitely up for that.

The Gift That Keeps on Giving

If you've ever been to a Southern Baptist Sunday School Christmas party, it is likely that you have been a participant in what is called, "A White Elephant Gift Exchange."

It was years ago that I was part of this holiday party game, but during that time I was never able to determine why it was named such, as I never saw a pachyderm, white or otherwise.

And now, thanks to the Internet, you and I both know more.

For those who aren't familiar with this party game, the object is quite simple: Bring the worst gift you can find and give it to someone else.

The rules for the white elephant gift exchange can vary as much as Monopoly (those hosting the game typically make the rules), but generally, you place your gift under the tree and people take turns selecting one to open.

After the first person opens one of their choosing, the next person can choose to either open another gift or take the one the first person opened. Each person can either pick a gift or steal a previously opened one, but once everyone has a gift, stolen or otherwise, the game is done.

The origin of this unusual holiday party exchange possibly dates back to the mid-1800s and may have included real white elephants.

Let's start with a definition. The Merriam-Webster online dictionary offers several, but these are the most relevant:

White Elephant

a: a property requiring much care and expense
and yielding little profit
b: an object no longer of value to its owner but
of value to others
c: something of little or no value

For the sake of this discussion, I'm going with
A and C: a property requiring much care and
expense and yielding little profit; and something
of little or no value.

After leaving the dictionary site, my research
migrated to The University of Google. I
discovered that the white elephant gift exchange
is also called a Yankee Swap in some parts of
the country. But, regardless of the name, as I
mentioned earlier, one legend says that it began
with a connection to real white elephants.

Allegedly, (meaning this is just as likely to be
made up as it is to be true) the King of Siam
would give albino elephants to the members of
his court that he didn't like. The cost of upkeep
for white elephants supposedly was expensive
and could bankrupt the recipient.

The modern version of this approach to gift
giving obviously doesn't include white
elephants or bankruptcy, but the goal is similar:

Give someone something you don't want, they don't want, and is hard to get rid of.

Over the years of participating in a white elephant gift exchange I've seen the things you'd typically expect, such as ugly Christmas sweaters (which, of course, is redundant), toilet plungers, and cheese graters. But, without a doubt, the all-time winner was the first year someone brought an antique breast pump. I say first time because this gift returned year after year.

Its first appearance went something like this:

(Person opens gift)

(Women burst out laughing)

(Men look at each other and ask, "What is that?")

I'm not sure which the women found funnier; the fact that there was an antique breast pump at a Southern Baptist Sunday School Christmas party, or that the men didn't have a clue what it was.

For the record, I'm fairly certain that it was the latter.

What I do know is that it kept resurfacing at subsequent parties and that I wound up with it at least once.

If there's anything women find more humorous than seeing a man who doesn't want to be holding an antique breast pump, holding an antique breast pump, I've yet to witness it.

Each year, the men would try to come up with a white elephant gift that would top an antique breast pump, but as you might imagine, we failed miserably.

I haven't participated in a white elephant gift exchange in many years, and honestly, I haven't missed it.

I also have no idea what happened to the aforementioned pump, but I'm hopeful that it was lost in an intense fire, run over by a road grader, or accidentally loaded onto a NASA mission to Alpha Centauri.

But, if you've been asked to participate in a white elephant gift exchange this year and needed an idea for the worst gift ever; you're welcome.

CHAPTER FIVE – SOMEONE'S IN THE KITCHEN

The Crock-Pot Crackpots

During a recent discussion with coworkers, someone asked me what was typically served every Sunday after church when I was a kid.

Of course, I said pot roast.

Pot roasts migrated from the oven to the Crock-Pot during my childhood. The Crock-Pot was and still is the perfect cooking appliance for a pot roast. It was also the original set-it-and-forget-it appliance.

Moms would get up in the morning and sear the roast in a cast iron skillet, then toss it and an accompaniment of potatoes, carrots and onions in the Crock-Pot, turn it on low, and the family would then head off to church. Returning to a house filled with the aroma of fresh roast beef was an amazing thing.

Today, we have grown accustomed to instant everything. But the Crock-Pot, a copyrighted name owned by a company called Rival that has now become a generic term like Kleenex and Coke, truly was a game changer.

That is, until the government got involved. Yes, you read that correctly. The government got involved in Crock-Pots and all other slow cookers.

And you know what happens when the government gets involved in something: It gets worse. And that's what has happened with Crock-Pots.

How I discovered this little tidbit of technological trivia all started with a Christmas gift a few years ago. We received a brand new Crock-Pot from a friend. Happy to receive the new slow cooker, we gave away our 1970s Rival model.

We should never have done that.

The first time we tried to use our new Crock-Pot, we noticed that it was boiling, even when it was set on low. Now, I'm by no means a scientist, but I'm pretty sure that boiling and slow cooker shouldn't be used in the same sentence.

Thinking that our new Crock-Pot was defective, I went online to see if there had been a recall on that make and model. Instead, I found online forums full of angry customers who had done the same thing we had. They got rid of their old cooker and got a new one.

From what I've been able to ascertain, at some point in the not-so-distant past, the government mandated that slow cookers had to boil food on the low setting. You can imagine what kind of pot roast that produces. Somehow, even though humans have survived for thousands of years by preparing our own food, the government felt it necessary to intervene.

My next stop online was eBay. I wanted to find the same model of Crock-Pot we had given away and buy it. What I found was that those who possessed the old Crock-Pots knew what they had, and they knew that they could charge accordingly. The one we wanted to get back was going for $79, plus shipping.

I closed my Internet browser and started scouring garage sales, estate sales, and junk shops for old Crock-Pots. I found several. I began picking them up for $5 or $10 each. Some were in fair shape, others were in great shape, but most just needed a good cleaning. I took my Crock-Pot search seriously because I wanted to make sure that as many of my family members who wanted one of the original good ones, got one.

Over the course of a couple of years, I acquired several vintage models. However, I never found the exact one we wanted, so to get the orange metal model, which has a removable pot and cheesy 1970s graphics, I wound up back on eBay and paid the premium price.

But, it was completely worth it. Now, we can get up in the morning and sear the roast in a cast iron skillet, then toss it and an accompaniment of potatoes, carrots and onions in the Crock-Pot, turn it on low, and return to a house filled with the aroma of fresh roast beef.

If I ever have the opportunity to cook for the government Crock-Pot crackpots who got involved in the slow-cooker business, I'll be sure to dig out the new one we got as a gift and fix them plenty of overcooked pork.

Still Cookin' After All These Years

A coworker recently mentioned that she and her family had bought a new home. Actually, it was new to them, but it was built in 1963 in what was then and is still now one of the city's most desirable neighborhoods.

What seemed like a typical workplace side conversation took a very positive turn when she mentioned that the appliances were all original. And they still worked.

No doubt, I'm a sucker for vintage anything, but I've always been drawn to antique appliances. The men and women who designed the early stoves, ovens, refrigerators, toasters, percolators, and other kitchen mainstays were, in my opinion, artists.

I challenge anyone to compare a stove made between the 1930s and 1960s to one made today and tell me that the modern stove looks better. It's like comparing a Cadillac made then to one made now.

Besides the fact that some thought actually went into the look and design of everything from toasters to cook tops, the older product lines were made in America and were solid. How solid is quite evident. My coworker isn't the only person who still has a functioning kitchen full of antique appliances. The Internet has pages dedicated to them.

As recently as 20 years ago, people were spending thousands of dollars to gut an older house, junk the appliances and replace them with new ones.

But, as with most things, tastes are cyclical. This is now the case with old appliances.

Not only are people proudly showing off their harvest gold, avocado green, and Brittany blue ovens, cook tops, and refrigerators, there is a cottage industry for replacement parts.

Need a replacement broiler element for your aqua-colored, 1960s oven? Try eBay or one of several other websites where what's called "new old stock" parts can be found. I stumbled across retrorenovation.com and discovered a great resource for those who love and use vintage appliances.

There are a number of companies there that offer parts, service advice and other help. And the assistance isn't limited to the kitchen. For those who use antique vacuum cleaners, oscillating fans, and lamps, there are resources for them too.

A group called The Old Appliance Club works to help folks find parts they need.

There's even a company that makes brand-new appliances that look like they were made during the Eisenhower administration. Northstar Appliances manufactures ovens, refrigerators, and even microwaves, that take a second look before you're sure that they're not 60 years old. There are also new small appliances that are made in the retro style. You can choose those – or the real deal – for your kitchen countertops. A surprising number of new, old stock coffee makers, toasters, blenders, mixers, and other unused items are still available.

Whether they were wedding gifts that were never used or a purchase that was just stored and forgotten in an attic or closet, one will never know. But, for those who want to stay with or return to the retro kitchen look, the options are now endless.

My wife and I use a 1960 percolator and a 1957 GE toaster every morning.

The percolator not only still works as reliably as the day it came out of the box, it makes better coffee than any modern drip model or a single-cup system. The toaster has a tray in the bottom for reheating, and a pop-up system in the top. I found multiple sites on the Internet that offer parts for both.

My coworker was nice enough to comply with my request to send some photos of her oven and cook top when she got home. The push-button oven looked just as I remember them from when I was a kid.

I was proud for her, but also a little jealous. She not only bought a great house, her kitchen was perfectly preserved and is still cooking up meals for her family.

What's cookin'? Turns out, when it comes to vintage kitchens, a whole lot.

The Pioneer Skillet

My momma's skillet and this columnist are featured in the fall issue of the Pioneer Woman Magazine.

Well, it used to be my momma's skillet. She gave it to me when I left home almost 40 years ago.

And there it is on page 72 (2017 Fall Issue – Pioneer Woman Magazine) of Ree Drummond's magazine.

If by chance, you aren't familiar with Ree Drummond (The Pioneer Woman), she has built a media empire that grew out of a blog she began writing in 2006. It chronicles her daily life with a husband and four children living on a large ranch in Oklahoma.

Her story is one of a metropolitan woman who married a cowboy. Her tales of adapting to her new life resonated with millions, and her world has grown to include a TV show, several books and cookbooks, and a mercantile in her hometown of Pawhuska, Oklahoma, among other things.

So, how does a guy living in East Texas wind up with a small feature in the magazine of one of the most popular women in America?

First, let me tell you about my skillet. It is nine inches in diameter and is old. How old, we don't know. From the limited information it provides and some online research I did, this piece of cast iron likely was made by one of two companies: Wagner or Griswold.

What I know for sure is that this skillet originally came from my dad's maternal grandmother and was used by my mom to prepare virtually every meal I ate growing up. I can recall being just the right height so that the cook top of my mom's gas stove was eye level for me. My mom would put some bacon renderings in that skillet and turn on the burner.

The flames would dance around the bottom of the skillet, and the grease would begin to sizzle.

My mom would then put sliced potatoes, breaded okra, or whatever else was on the menu, into that piece of cast iron. I can still see that kitchen in my mind, smell the smells, and hear my mom talking to me as she cooked for us.

When I was a child, there were three things that were part of every meal. We always had fried potatoes, white gravy, and homemade biscuits. The first two were made in that skillet. The biscuits were baked on a cookie sheet in the oven.

Often at dinner or supper (there is no lunch in Arkansas) my mom would make me a fried baloney sandwich, which was blackened to perfection in that skillet.

I was always interested in learning how to cook, and my mom would show me how to make basic things. As I got older (around 11 or 12), I decided one Friday after school that I would cook dinner and clean the house for my mom before she got home.

I don't remember what I cooked, but what I do remember is that I used an SOS Pad to remove all of what I thought was built up on that skillet.

When my mom got home and I proudly showed her how clean her skillet was, that's when I learned about how cast-iron skillets are seasoned and that the buildup was supposed to be there.

I never cleaned the skillet that way again.

In spite of my misstep, my mother bequeathed me that skillet when I moved out after high school. I've had it with me ever since.

Back to The Pioneer Woman. My wife and I are big fans. One evening we were watching her TV show, which featured her using her cast iron and bragging about how much she loved it.

At the time, I just happened to be logged on to the social media network, Twitter. So, I sent Ree Drummond a Tweet, thanking her for highlighting my favorite cookware.

Now, most of the time when you send a Tweet to a celebrity, it's likely that they never read it, much less respond or have someone respond to it.

But, a few months later, I received an email through my website. It was from a lady named Lauren who worked for Hearst Publications in New York City. She told me that Ree was launching a new magazine, and that my Tweet had caught someone's eye (I have no idea if it was Ree or someone else) and asked me to expound on my love of cast iron.

I wrote a short bit, similar to the one I just shared with you in this column and sent it to her. A short time later, she emailed again and asked for pictures. One of the skillets and one of me. She also asked about my plans for the skillet.

I wrote her back and said that my mom's skillet, along with my now much larger collection of cast iron, will go to our grandchildren.

I received word that I had been selected to be included in the second issue, which is the fall edition. Other cast iron lovers were also selected. I share a page with them.

If you want to buy a copy, you'll need to back order online. My mom bought all of the copies that Wal Mart had.

The Chicken Fried Stakes

There is a short list of things in the South that you'd better know how to do correctly, or someone will quickly say, "Bless your heart."

Making a good chicken fried steak is near the top of that list. There's a lot at stake when it comes to claiming you make a good one. Pun intended.

For the most part, cooks south of the Mason-Dixon line know how to make a decent chicken fried steak. Those who don't, know which restaurants do.

No self-respecting Southerner would ever misrepresent their chicken fried steak skills, any more than they would claim to be able to make sweet tea without brewing a pitcher that can actually back that statement up.

An excellent chicken fried steak requires the following: Flour, eggs, whole milk, salt and pepper, and (here's the most important part) flat iron steak run through the tenderizer. At least twice.

Flat iron steak, also called top blade steak, is allegedly called such because it looks like a piece of flat iron. It comes from the shoulder of the cow and is used in many other dishes, including fajitas and Asian foods.

I verified the right cut of meat with the world's most renowned meat expert: my cousin Roger.

Roger has been a butcher since Reagan was in the White House and, trust me, he knows his beef. Once, in the early '80s, he was stuck at my house during an ice storm and he turned a package of steaks and a can of pepper into a delicious, cast iron-seared delicacy.

So, if you're going to make your own chicken fried steak, go with flat iron steak. If you have to get your fix at a restaurant, do your homework first on who has the real deal.

Many restaurants try and woo you by claiming that they have the largest chicken fried steak. Do not be deceived by these purveyors of less-than-stellar cutlets. This is one instance where size doesn't matter.

Just because someone prepares you something that is served on a pizza tray and smothered in gravy does not mean that it is good. In many cases, it's not even edible.

I'm not sure if it's still in business, but there used to be a restaurant in Fort Worth that had a menu that included a chicken fried steak that weighed over 5 pounds, came with French fries and gravy, a salad, and other items, and was free if you could eat it all. If you couldn't finish everything, you owed them $70 bucks.

That didn't include the cost of the tip, or the quadruple bypass you'd need later on. I never tried it, so I don't know if it was good or not, but I'm not sure you can tell whether something tastes good after consuming 5 pounds of anything.

The best chicken fried steak I've ever eaten in a restaurant was, hands down, at Miss Mac's Café in Ashdown, Arkansas.

It was actually just called "Mac's Café," but since Miss Mac always seemed to be behind the counter or in the kitchen of this hometown truck stop, we all just called it "Miss Mac's."

She didn't actually call it a chicken fried steak, she called it a "Hot Steak Sandwich." It was served on a piece of white diner china (that's right, diner, not dinner) and included a chicken fried steak served on a piece of toast, smothered in gravy, with another piece of toast cut in half and placed on each side of the steak, and it also came with French fries, a salad, and a glass of sweet tea.

The salad dressing was a mixture of her own design that was so good, we'd put it on crackers while we waited for our meal. Outside of a home-cooked chicken fried steak, Miss Mac had every other restaurant beat. And remember what I said about saying you know how to make sweet tea? Miss Mac could back that up, too.

I can't remember what we paid for that Hot Steak Sandwich, but I want to say it was around $2.75. Many a late night was spent in Mac's eating that wonderful meal. I'd give just about anything for a time machine to take me back there for just one more visit.

But, in the absence of an H.G. Wells invention, we'll have to settle for making our own.

My cousin Roger was nice enough to let me interrupt him while he was watching the Astros game, and he gave me permission to share his chicken fried steak recipe, which he got from his momma and swears that she makes it better than him.

I believe that. Here it is. You can thank me later.

Cousin Roger and Aunt Gail's Chicken Fried Steak recipe:

Ingredients:

Package of Iron Flank Steak
1 cup whole milk
1 1/2 cups of Flour

1 Egg
Salt
Pepper

Instructions: Start with flat iron steak that has
been tenderized several times. Place 1 1/2 cups
of flour on plastic wrap. In a shallow bowl, beat
1 egg and 1 cup of milk together. Sprinkle meat
with salt and black pepper. First, dip meat in
flour, then milk egg mixture, then back in flour.
Fry in oil that has been heated to 350 degrees
until done.

A Cup of Joe

Joe DiMaggio was great for baseball, but he was
bad for coffee.

The man who got a hit in 56 straight games in
1941 and married Marilyn Monroe, could do no
wrong in the eyes of most people. I agree,
except for one thing: He killed the percolator.

Prior to 1972, most American households used a
percolator to brew their morning beans. But,
that year, two bad things happened: Richard
Nixon was re-elected, and the Mr. Coffee drip-
brewing system debuted.

117

I'm sure there will be some who read these words and consider my condemnation of Mr. Coffee as java heresy, but I would argue that if you've never had great percolator coffee, quite simply, you likely have been the victim of Mr. DiMaggio's marketing influence and/or an absence of percolator opportunity.

For those unfamiliar with how a percolator brews coffee, there is a pot with a handle, and often, a glass bubble in the center of the lid where you can see the coffee perking. Inside, there is a metal stem that sits in a hole in the bottom of the pot, through which the water travels to land in a grounds basket. Small holes in the basket allow the perked coffee to drain.

Percolators obviously need a heat source. This can come from a stovetop for models that aren't electric, or from a heating element for countertop plug-in models.

The latter is what I grew up with. When my parents married in the early 1960s, they acquired a Regal Easy Go percolator. As a child, I awoke each day to the sound and smell of that percolator.

In 1970, two years before their Mr. Coffee debuted, two guys in Cleveland named Vincent Marotta and Samuel Glazer put together a

company and hired some engineers to design the
new brewing system. They called it new, but 13
years earlier in 1957, the Bunn system began
making coffee with the same drip design.

The only difference that I can see between a Mr.
Coffee and a Bunn is that with a Bunn brewer
you have to pour the water into the top when
you're ready to make it. The Mr. Coffee allows
you to pour the water in, but it won't start
making coffee until you turn on the power
switch.

As a young kid, before Mr. Coffee was even
heard of, I saw lots of Bunns in diners and truck
stops. The upside of this drip system is that they
work fast. I'd watch waitresses constantly
making new pots of coffee and refill the
trucker's cups, all while taking orders,
delivering food, and fending off the pick-up
lines of the male patrons.

It reminded me of the guy at the circus who kept
10 plates spinning at the same time on the top of
some really tall sticks without dropping and
breaking any of the plates.

So, I don't think that the Mr. Coffee was that
new of an idea or even that different of a design.

But, what Mr. Marotta and Glazer did better than the Bunn Company was that they had the idea to make a much smaller version of the drip system that would fit on a kitchen counter. They also knew Joe DiMaggio.

The argument that was made to claim that a drip system was better than percolator coffee was that percolator coffee was too strong and bitter.

There was truth to this claim, but there was a reason it could be too strong and bitter. People left the percolator sitting on the burner on the stove or left the electric ones plugged in to keep the coffee hot.

Well, naturally, if you do that, your coffee will go from original to extra crispy in short order. This was before microwaves, so reheating coffee wasn't quick or easy like it is now.

My grandfather was a blacksmith and he would trek from his shop to the house and back several times a day to refill his cup. By the end of the day, the smell of the coffee was quite pungent. But he was used to it and knew nothing different.

Convincing people that you could make coffee that didn't turn into motor oil was an easy sell. According to the Mr. Coffee info on Wikipedia,

Joe DiMaggio was hired as the pitchman in 1973, and by 1974, over 1 million Mr. Coffee devices had taken their place on America's kitchen countertops and the percolators were relegated to storage.

That's how I wound up with my first percolator. For years, I was one of the many who drank the Mr. Coffee Kool-Aid. I started drinking coffee when I went to work in radio in the late '70s. We had a Mr. Coffee at the station, so when I got my own apartment, that's what I bought.

But about 10 years ago, I stopped at an estate sale. There was a beautiful percolator that was obviously old, but well cared for. Out of nostalgia, I asked the price. So, for 50 cents, I went home with a Universal Coffeematic. My online research showed that it was made in 1960 in Connecticut.

It was 4 in the afternoon when I came home with it, but I cleaned it up and decided to see if it worked. My wife and I tried a cup of the coffee. It was amazing.

We had another cup.

I took our Mr. Coffee and relegated it to storage. I even went on eBay and bought an identical percolator just so we'd have a backup. The coffee is that good.

The trick to drinking percolator coffee is to unplug it when it's done perking and pour the coffee into a good thermos. That way, it doesn't turn into Quaker State 10W-30.

My mom even gave me her old percolator. So, our backup percolator has a backup.

Now, Joe is once again with Marilyn, and my wife and I have rediscovered the percolator.

Things are back as they should be.

Vintage Bowls

We were watching one of my wife's favorite cooking shows when she noticed a set of colored bowls the woman on the television was using.

"My mother used to have a set of bowls just like that!" she said. "I always loved those bowls. I wonder whatever happened to them? I wonder if she still has them? I'd love to have a set of those. They bring back so many memories!"

Before she had finished the last two sentences, I was already on eBay on the iPad, quietly searching for the set of four. I found the next-to-the-smallest, the red one, first.

I had to do a double take. It had to be that the person who listed this bowl for sale must've accidentally put an extra zero on the asking price.

The next bowl I found was the largest one, the yellow one, by a different seller. After looking at the price, I was now sure that the extra zeroes weren't an accident.

Holy smokes. Why are these bowls so expensive? I thought.

And then it hit me. For the same reason that my wife wanted these bowls, so did millions of other women. They wanted to buy back part of their youth. The part that connected them to their mothers. The part that connected them to youthful happiness. The part that connected them to simpler and more pleasing times.

Talking with her mother by phone, she said that she'd acquired her set of bowls in the early 1950s.

Before I began searching for the other two bowls, the green and blue ones, I had made up my mind that nothing was going to stop me from finding all four of these bowls, in good condition, and surprising my wife with them.

The only decision that I was going to have to make regarding the acquisition of these Pyrex prizes was whether I'd need to plan a bank heist or take out a second mortgage.

Without my wife knowing, my search continued. I found a handful of sellers who had the whole set, but the case with all of the sets was there was at least one bowl, sometimes two or more, that had a scratch, chip, or some other blemish or damage. Even with imperfections, these bowls were still selling for what I thought was a lot of money.

So, my strategy was to locate the best bowl of each color and then privately message the seller and negotiate a sensible price.

I quickly discovered that it would be easier for me to get a job as George Clooney's stunt double than to convince a woman who owns a vintage piece of Pyrex to sell it to me for less than she thinks its worth. And so, paying the asking price for each bowl is exactly what I did.

After finding, ordering, and sending the money for each bowl, I arranged with each seller to ship the item in such a way that I could clandestinely pick up each one, hide it, and then give the set to my wife at the time of my choosing.

In the meantime, I decided to do a bit of research on these bowls. These Pyrex mixing bowls are what many people refer to as "The 400 Series." The bowls made in the 1950s and later included a number on the bottom. The smallest, the blue one, is 401, the red one is 402, the green is 403, and the yellow is 404.

The bowls made prior to the 1950s did not have numbers on them. The bottom was stamped, "T.M. REG." So, if you come across a set of these bowls with no numbers, hang on to them. You've got some money there.

Also, on the numbered bowls, they include the capacity of each. The smallest bowl holds a pint and a half. The largest bowl holds a gallon.

While I was at it, I decided to also locate and buy a bowl like my mom used when I was growing up. It is also a Pyrex bowl, but it's clear in the bottom and painted green on the outside.

Hey, I figured if I was getting my wife four bowls like the ones her mom had, I could get one like my mom had for myself.

The bowls all arrived separately, yet somehow, I was able to keep my wife from seeing them and I hid them in the closet until I was ready to present her with all of them.

She was beyond pleased. She may have even teared up a little when I gave them to her. She uses them often, for everything from salads, to dips, to mixing ingredients for things she's making.

My wife is pretty protective of these bowls. It's not that I'm not allowed to use them, it's just that I get "the eye" whenever I do. I know that that means if I break one, I'll be sleeping in the Prius for a while.

So, I rarely use her vintage Pyrex bowls. It's a lot more fun to watch her use them. It connects her to her youth, her mother, happiness, and a simpler, more pleasing time.

The only thing that might make my wife happier would be if I actually could pass for George Clooney's stunt double.

At least she has the bowls.

126

CHAPTER SIX – FAMOUS FOLKS

Name-Dropping

Most old-school celebrities are just regular folks.

There are very few celebrities I'll spend money to see, but Jay Leno made the list.

We sat in the audience waiting for him to take the stage, and when he did, he didn't disappoint. He's one of the few comedians left who can be non-stop funny for 90 minutes without being vulgar.

We didn't get to meet Jay, but he seems like a nice guy. He has that reputation in the show business community.

As we left the venue to grab a bite to eat, I thought about the celebrities and famous people I have met. In my former career in broadcasting, I met a lot of well-known people. It was part of the job.

Singers were always touring to promote and sell albums, writers were pushing books, actors were hawking a movie or TV series or trying to raise awareness for a charity, and politicians were trying to get re-elected.

As a seventeen-year-old just starting out, my first few celebrity encounters were nerve-wracking. On live radio, I had to interview Mel Tillis. Fortunately, he was very nice and accommodating. I'm sure he sensed my nervousness and tried to help me out. I'm guessing it's probably the only time in his career when the interviewer stuttered more than he did.

But, the more well known people I met and interviewed, the more it became obvious that they were just regular people who had worked hard to succeed at what they did. Most of them were very appreciative for what you were doing to help promote their career.

When the Judds first hit the scene, they had one hit under their belt. I interviewed Wynonna backstage at a community college auditorium. She and I were about the same age, and it seemed as if one kid was interviewing another. She was cordial and unassuming.

Just two years later, she and her mom would be one of the biggest acts in country music.

Randy Travis surprised me. He was promoting a new album and called me from the set of a movie he was filming. I was in the studio doing my show, and the interview was live. He stayed on for about half an hour, and then talked to me off-air for another 45 minutes.

A genuinely nice guy who was grateful for his success. I feel bad for how things have turned out for his health and pray that he will improve. I met and interviewed the beautiful singer Lorrie Morgan. She made me stutter, too.

Vice President Dan Quayle was the antithesis of how the left in the press portrayed him. He was very articulate and obviously one of the smartest people in the room. I met him when he came to town trying to help him and his boss keep their jobs in the White House. He looked more like a movie star than a politician. Striking in looks and talked to you as if you were old friends.

President Bill Clinton was the master of interacting with people. I met him when he was still the Governor of Arkansas. I've never seen anyone else work a room full of people like he does. All of his faults aside, he went out of his way to be nice.

Remember Jerry Mathers? Beaver Cleaver from TV? He makes the top-five list of nicest celebrities I've worked with. I say worked with, because he spent two days in town on a promotional tour. I was assigned to him to make sure everything went OK, so that included picking him up and taking him where he needed to go. One evening, he addressed a crowd of 800 people and then stayed for photos and autographs of everyone who wanted one. Later, at a restaurant, he greeted everyone who approached him, even though they were interrupting his meal.

I was even able to interview one of my idols. Mel Blanc may not be a name you immediately recognize, but you know his work. He did the voices of over 1,000 cartoon characters, including Bugs Bunny, Daffy Duck, Yosemite Sam, Sylvester, Tweety, and many more for Warner Brothers.

I talked to him by phone in 1984, just five years before he passed. He was so kind and generous. There's nothing quite like hearing Bugs Bunny say your name.

If there's one thing I miss about broadcasting, it's the interaction with the famous people who turn out to be just regular folks.

I didn't get a chance to meet Jay Leno, but Jay, if you're reading this, you rank right up there with Mel in the idol category.

Filling in the Blanc

I waited six months to talk to him. That's what his receptionist told me the wait time was for an interview when I called his Beverly Hills office in early 1984.

Since he was my childhood idol, I was willing to wait the required one-half year to have him on my radio show. And wait, I did.

"Alright," I said. "Six months from today is August 8th. What time should I call?"

"Noon," she answered.

"Noon it is," I responded. And then I confirmed the two-hour time difference.

I would call Mel Blanc at 2 p.m. on August 8, 1984. I wrote it in my daily planner.

My excitement was unusual. Part of working in the radio business and doing a talk show is scheduling and interviewing celebrities, politicians, and other public figures. Most didn't impress me or make me nervous, but this one did.

I was going to talk to the Man of a Thousand Voices. The man who created the voices of

131

Bugs Bunny, Daffy Duck, Yosemite Sam, The Roadrunner, Foghorn Leghorn, and many other characters in the Warner Brothers Looney Toons animated shorts.

This was a big deal. And I told everyone for the next six months.

Rewind a moment to two decades prior. It was the 1960s, and my Saturday mornings were filled with Cap'n Crunch and a large, RCA color console television that was tuned to *The Bugs Bunny Show*.

The fact that it debuted on television the same year I was born was not a coincidence, in my opinion.

I devoured every single Looney Toon. I learned the dialogue. And I learned the voices. I was so good at them that during rainy days in gym class, the other guys would have me recreate an entire cartoon while we sat on the faded, uncomfortable bleachers at Brown Junior High School.

No one ever told me that Mel Blanc had such a unique voice, that you weren't supposed to be able to sound like him. I had seen Rich Little impersonate real people, so I just figured that anyone could do voices.

So, I practiced and practiced.

Did I sound just like him? Of course not, but junior high boys can be brutal. If I hadn't been close, I would have been treated like junior high boys treat a bad performance.

I decided that that's what I wanted to do when I grew up: I wanted to voice cartoons like the guy who did Bugs Bunny. But, who was he?

I read the credits on each cartoon, and Mel Blanc was the only name listed for "voice characterizations." That's how I first learned who he was. But there was no Internet, and the library offered little in the way of information.

My father explained to me that Mel Blanc had been around since the early 1930s. In addition to getting the job as Warner Brothers' exclusive voice talent, he also did a lot of work on radio programs, and later, early television shows.

He worked a lot with Jack Benny, playing everything from Jack's long-suffering French violin teacher to the voice of Benny's old Maxwell automobile.

So, on rare occasions, I would see Mel Blanc on television, but I still knew little about him.

When I was 17, I got a job at the local radio station in my hometown. It was there that I began honing my interview skills. After a few celebrity interviews, it occurred to me that if I could interview famous country singers, why couldn't I interview Mel Blanc?

So, that became my goal. But, working on the local station, where the hospital admissions and dismissals report, the fishing show and the local preachers were the standard fare, there really wasn't a place for an interview with Bugs Bunny.

So, I filed it away but never let it go. I was going to interview Mel Blanc one day. While I had him on the line, maybe I could hit him up for a job.

A few years passed. I married and had kids. I also moved to a bigger radio market.

I would do the Looney Toons voices for my sons. They thought that it was normal for a dad to sound like their favorite cartoons. Their visiting friends assured them that it was not normal.

The radio station I worked for changed its format. As listeners migrated from the AM to the FM dial for music, AM stations were scrambling to find an audience. So, talk radio was born.

I was put on the afternoon drive slot and did one of the first p.m. drive talk shows in Texarkana, Texas. This was before Rush Limbaugh, Sean Hannity, and others who are now mainstays.

In the early days of talk radio, anything went – within reason, of course. So, the local police safety officer did traffic reports, we had call-ins from listeners on current topics, and there was room for interviews.

I had four hours a day to fill, so my general manager was pretty lenient as far as whom I booked.

I mentioned to him one day that I was going to book Mel Blanc.

"Mel Blanc?" he said. "You really think you can get him on your show?"

No one thought had I should be able to do the Looney Toons voices, so getting Mel to do an interview shouldn't be a problem either, right?

"Yes, six months from now is August 8, 1984, at noon, my time," Mr. Blanc's receptionist said.

So, at the agreed-upon time, I called. And it wasn't the same receptionist. She had nothing on the books about an interview with some guy from Texarkana.

I was not giving up.

"Ma'am," I said. "Down here in Texas, we honor our commitments. I'm sure that Mr. Blanc wouldn't want to disappoint the listeners. I told them all yesterday that he was going to be on the show today. There'll sure be a lot of disappointed little kids."

The main disappointed little kid was going to be me. I'd waited my entire 21 years for this moment.

"One moment," she said.

A few moments later, I heard an unmistakable voice come on the line.

The next 11 minutes and 39 seconds were the most memorable of my 25 years in broadcasting. He was nice to me and answered all of my questions.

He even said my name in Bugs Bunny's voice.

I thanked him and hung up. The interview aired that day.

I never asked him about working for him. I didn't have the nerve. But, I did go to Hollywood five years later and tried to get my foot in the door at Warner Brothers. I had no luck.

Mel Blanc died in 1989. Out of all of the celebrities I've interviewed, and there were a lot of them, Mel was the highlight of my career.

I kept the cassette tape of our conversation.

Before I sat down to write this, I dug through my things and I found it. I drug my cassette deck out of the closet, hooked it up, and transferred it to my computer.

I'll end this chapter in my best Mel Blanc voice:

"The, Th, The, Th, The, uh…That's all, folks!"

Not That Dirty of a Job

If you don't know who Mike Rowe is, you should look him up online. Mr. Rowe represents what the average man in America used to resemble only a few short years ago.

He's levelheaded, smart, tries to avoid talking about politics or religion, and he is doing what he can to help other people.

Mike tried several different jobs (300 according to his website) between 2003 and 2012 when he starred in and worked on the TV show *Dirty Jobs* on The Discovery Channel.

On *Dirty Jobs*, he worked as a bat cave scavenger, roadkill cleaner, sewer inspector, leather tanner, sheep castrator, hot tar roofer, and several other professions that virtually all of the rest of mankind would never do.

Not all of the jobs were awful. He also tried being a wine maker and locomotive builder. I wouldn't mind giving those two a shot.

Through his charity, the mikeroweWORKS Foundation, Mike helps people who want to learn a skill. Specifically, learn a skill for a job that exists. Or, as my grandparents used to call it, "learning a trade."

His website goes into detail about how his organization works with people who are interested in doing something other than going to college. These are folks who want an honest living, but don't want to have to study Dante and the French Revolution to make said living.

Mike makes the point, and I completely agree with him on this, that too many people are going to college and getting degrees for jobs that don't exist.

Consequently, (and this is me talking now, not Mr. Rowe) we have a lot of young people who are still living with their parents instead of on their own.

These poor kids are coming out of school with a mountain of debt from student loans and they can't find work, much less work that pays back their loans and helps them pay rent and eat.

I grew up in a blue-collar family. My dad's father was a blacksmith. My mom's father delivered ice before people had electricity. Both sides of my family learned how to do many different jobs. Not because they wanted to, but because they had to.

Welding, farming, and raising livestock were just some of the jobs that my family members mastered.

Today, most of us do very little in the way of learning a trade. Not that there's anything wrong with a college degree. I have a degree and was the first in my family to acquire one.

But, I agree with Mike Rowe. There are job openings out there that business owners are having trouble filling, so why not at least offer the trades as a career option?

If people would be open-minded about possible career opportunities, they might just discover that there's a whole new world out there waiting for them.

Let me bring back up my college degree and the profession of welding as a comparison.

My degree is in journalism. As glamorous as working as a reporter might seem, you would be quite surprised at how little reporters make.

When I got into the field of journalism in the late 1970s, I worked in radio. One of the many hats I wore was, when needed, serving as a local reporter. My starting salary was $2.20 an hour and all of the bad coffee I wanted. Granted, that was almost 40 years ago, but reporters don't make a lot more than that these days.

Many of the reporters you see on television in small to medium markets are making less than $30K a year. Some, closer to $20K a year.

Compare that with a trained welder, who does not need a degree and who, according to Mike Rowe's website, profoundlydisconnected.com, could earn over $100K a year. Welders can train in as few as nine months, and if they want to be a traveling industrial pipe welder, they can earn as much as $185K a year.

Underwater welders can make $1,000 a day.

I know I couldn't make $1,000 a day as a writer, but I'd try underwater writing for that kind of dough.

My point of writing this column on this Labor Day weekend is twofold: I would love for more people to consider a profession they may not have thought of previously, and I'd like for more people to check out Mike Rowe and his foundation.

Mike is trying to make a difference in America's job market at a time when most other folks are arguing about politics and religion.

141

His podcasts on his website at mikerowe.com are a joy, quite reminiscent of Paul Harvey. His voice is the envy of most announcers I know, and his wisdom is endless.

What say we skip the discussions of politics and religion and try harder to be like Mike?

Funny Has Fallen

Comedians aren't what they used to be.

This became quite obvious when my wife and I recently sat down to watch a 1969 episode of "The Dick Cavett Show." A local channel is airing the program, which originally was on ABC's late-night schedule in the 1960s and '70s, but you also can watch it on YouTube.

The guest on this particular broadcast was Groucho Marx.

During his career, which spanned over seven decades and ended just prior to his death in 1977 at age 86, Groucho had no comedic peer. In my opinion, he still doesn't.

His early career was built with a vaudeville and stage act with his real-life brothers, Harpo,

Chico, Gummo, and Zeppo. The Marx Brothers made the transition to films, but it was after Gummo and Zeppo left the act that Groucho, Harpo, and Chico found real fame.

Movies such as A Night at the Opera, A Day at the Races, and Duck Soup are classics and show just how funny truly talented people can be.

Later, Groucho gave up the act and went solo. He enjoyed success hosting the quiz show, You Bet Your Life on first, radio, then television.

His later years were spent making the talk-show circuit, most often appearing on Cavett's show.

Marx's unbelievable wit was filled with ad-libs, sarcasm, and double-entendres, but he rarely went over the line.

Most of today's comedians go straight for the dirtiest or most vulgar thing they can think of. I'm by no means a prude, but when someone has to rely on profanity and off-color comments, it doesn't tell me they're funny, it tells me that they're not very smart.

True wit takes a high level of intelligence and mental acuity that few in the entertainment world possess these days. Many of the alleged comedians I see these days are just not funny.

Consider these Groucho quotes:

"Outside of a dog, a book is a man's best friend. Inside of a dog, it's too dark to read."

"The secret of life is honesty and fair dealing. If you can fake that, you've got it made."

"Man does not control his own fate. The women in his life do that for him."

"A child of five would understand this. Send someone to fetch a child of five."

"I've had a perfectly wonderful evening, but this wasn't it."

These are just a few of Groucho's brilliant quips.

As we watched Dick Cavett host Groucho on his show (I say host, because no one ever interviewed Groucho, they just got out of his way), it became obvious that we have lost not only true comedic talents, we've also lost skilled and intelligent talk show hosts.

I've always felt that Cavett, even though he won three Emmy Awards, never received the accolades he deserved. Don't get me wrong,

Johnny Carson was excellent, but Dick was in a different category. Cavett and his guests, for the most part, were far more cerebral than guests on other similar shows.

Cavett started out as an actor and comedy writer, and prior to getting his own talk show, he worked for Carson. Writing jokes for Carson's monologue and for Carson's predecessor, Jack Parr, served Cavett well when he later went in front of the camera.

Watching Cavett and Groucho interact was like watching two Olympic fencers nailing their marks with every thrust.

Late night TV hosts now do car karaoke. It is painfully obvious how far funny has fallen.

When the program ended, my wife and I agreed that there just isn't the level of talent out there that there was all those years ago. Watching the recording of the 1969 broadcast, which is now almost 50 years old, made me lament what we no longer have.

Groucho passed a few years after this episode aired, but Dick Cavett is still alive. I'm going to find an address for him and send him a thank-you letter. I will thank him for his brilliance, which we can all still enjoy, and for bringing back funny.

Even if it was only for an hour.

Memories of Mayberry

I've been thinking about Andy Griffith a lot lately. And I have Danny Thomas to thank for it.

I spend a lot of time trolling YouTube – the Internet website that allows anyone from large corporations to the average guy like me to upload videos.

Recently, I came across an Andy Griffith episode I'd never seen. For those of us who grew up watching the goings on of The Andy Griffith Show, finding an episode that we didn't know existed is comparable to Harrison Ford finding the real Ark.

But to clarify, the show I ran across in the wee hours of the morning on YouTube wasn't an episode of The Andy Griffith Show at all. Sure, Sheriff Andy Taylor was in it, and so was his son, Opie. Even Aunt Bee was there. Except, she wasn't Aunt Bee. She played the part of a

146

town widow. And the town drunk wasn't named Otis, nor was it the actor who played Otis.

What I had found was a program that would later lead to The Andy Griffith Show. It was an episode of The Danny Thomas Show that contained a show-within-a-show that introduced us to the town where we would all one day wish we could live: Mayberry.

In this episode, Danny Thomas ran a stop sign and was stopped by Andy. I won't recap the entire show, but suffice it to say, many jokes were written around Thomas – the rich, big city celebrity – being locked up and stuck in a town full of what Danny perceived to be uncultured, Southern rednecks.

By the end of the episode, Danny realized that judging people was a bad idea and that the folks in Andy's town were wise and fair.

Even though it was an episode of The Danny Thomas Show, it was the roadmap that led to what arguably would become the quintessential American television program that represented the best of who we were in the 1960s.

I devoured this heretofore-unknown slice of tasty Mayberry pie.

As a kid, I watched The Andy Griffith Show and I haven't stopped since then. But the exuberance I felt seeing this "lost" episode made me evaluate why I, and virtually every other person from my generation, loved this program so much.

For those of us who grew up in small-town USA, the answer is simple. Every character on that program represents someone we know or knew. And the relationships between the characters are familiar because they were also ours.

The relationship between Andy and Deputy Barney Fife (who in the early episodes we find out are related; cousins it is revealed) is symbolic of many similar family dynamics I've known. The family member who is unnecessarily overly self-assured is adopted by a different one who is generous with creative, corrective support.

We've all been Barney at one point or another in our lives.

We've all had an Aunt Bee (if we're lucky, more than one Aunt Bee), who was always there for us, oftentimes with a home-cooked meal and a hug.

Most of us have had a Floyd the barber in our life. That eclectic person may have been a barber, but instead could just as easily have been our next-door neighbor, mechanic, or friend.

I don't know about you, but I certainly have had a friend like Ernest T. Bass. Especially during my high school years. Some of my friends would likely argue that I was their Ernest T. Bass.

Other characters on the show, including Thelma Lou, Goober, Gomer, and the often referenced but never seen, Juanita and the phone operator Sarah, all could correlate to a person who was part of our world.

That's what made that show so relatable. Even though the writers and actors were all Hollywood folk, they somehow were able to connect with the average men and women spread across the country. The scenarios of each episode were simple, but when paired with the characters, they became relatable. And they still are today.

The Andy Griffith Show was so well done, that it's never left the air, and is still running in reruns some 50 years after Andy turned in his badge and Barney moved to Raleigh. They

149

made Mayberry seem so pleasant and real that we still want to see what's going on there.

The truth is, Mayberry didn't exist, even when the Andy Griffith Show was on the air. Griffith himself said that the show was set in the 1960s but was meant to be reminiscent of the 1930s. No town was as perfect as Mayberry then, and it certainly isn't now.

But it's about as close to a perfect town as most of us can ever get.

Doobie Brothers Still Rock

When I first picked up a guitar in 1970, my fingers didn't make the sounds I wanted to hear. But I knew that if I kept trying, I could learn to play the songs I heard on the radio.

I was eight.

My teacher's name was Mike and it was in his room in his parent's home that I learned the foundations of what makes the guitar an amazing instrument.

At first, it was daunting. I was forming the chords with my left hand and holding the pick and strumming with my right on a guitar that was almost as big as I was. The '50s era red and black acoustic belonged to my dad. The neck was wide, and the strings were thick, but with blisters on my fingers, I kept going.

At age 10, a song came on the radio that had an opening riff so infectious, I was determined to learn it. That song was "China Grove," by the Doobie Brothers. The crackle of my AM radio accented the song as it rode the late-night waves from WLS in Chicago to my small bedroom in Southwest Arkansas.

Gosh, I loved that song.

By age 14, I was playing in a garage band. In the 1970s, every high school had at least one group of four guys who were able to convince their mothers to take turns lugging them and their gear from one house to another to practice.

More often than not, Doug, Paul, Keith and I would practice at my house. I'm not sure if that was because we had a large game room with doors that served as protective barriers for my mom in the house and our neighbors on our street, or if it was just easier than my mom having to fill the trunk of her 1971 Buick Electra 225 Limited with my gear and take me somewhere else and then pick me up.

Our band began by learning "Johnny B. Goode," "Jailhouse Rock," and other rock standards, but we eventually learned "China Grove." I was very happy.

At age 17, I got my first job as a radio DJ. Our local station, KMLA (the K being a letter that virtually all stations west of the Mississippi start with, and MLA stood for "Millwood Lake Area"), hired me to work from 8 p.m. until midnight.

Two years later, the rock station in nearby Texarkana, KTFS, brought me on for the same shift.

One of my favorite things to do at both stations was to cue up the vinyl record, fire off the local station ID at the top of the hour, hit the start switch on the turntable, and play "China Grove."

"It's Ten-oh-five at 14-KTFS, Solid as A Rock. And here are the Doobies, and 'China Grove.'"

"...*When the sun comes up on a sleepy little town, down around San Antone. And the folks are rising for another day. Round about their home...*"

At age 20 while working at KTFS, the owner gave me tickets to see the Doobie Brothers perform in Dallas at the now-gone Reunion Arena. Jim was a nice guy. He knew how much I loved that band, and at the time, they were on their farewell tour.

The highlight of the concert for me was hearing "China Grove."

Around the same time that the Doobies were breaking up, so was the band I was in. I mothballed my guitars and amps, got married, had kids, finished college, and held real jobs.

My parents, along with most other sensible people, never really considered playing in bands or working in radio as real jobs. For the most part, they were right.

But after I left radio, I began working with a couple of guys who played guitar. We began to get together and play the old favorites. We took turns playing at each other's houses, but most often, we wound up at my house. I'm not sure if that was because we lived in the country and had doors and distance that could protect my wife and the neighbors, or if it was because my buddies' wives had a low pain tolerance.

Either way, I'd always try to slide in at least the opening riff to "China Grove" during each jam session.

After a few years apart, the Doobie Brothers reunited and began touring again.

Knowing how much I love the band, recently, my boss bought me a ticket and invited me to go with him to see the Doobies when they came through town.

Our seats were excellent. About seven rows back from center stage.

The lady who did the introduction surprised us. She said that we could take pictures and shoot video with our phones. And so I did.

The band took the stage and they rocked it. Almost 36 years had passed since I last saw the Doobies and they sounded as great as ever.

I kept my phone ready and hit record just as they fired off "China Grove."

When I got home, I wasn't sure what kind of audio quality I would have; but after uploading the video to my iPad and then to Facebook, I was very surprised at how great it sounded.

I made a post to Facebook to share this Classic Rock greatness with others. And I did it in my best, dusted-off radio DJ voice from days gone by. If you'll allow me, I'd like to also do that for you now.

"…Its Twelve-Oh-five at my house. And here are the Doobie Brothers, on my iPad…with 'China Grove.'"

CHAPTER SEVEN – COLLECTORS' ITEMS

Comics Were Super, Man

Comic books were a big part of my childhood.

As a preteen, my comic books went virtually everywhere with me. I say virtually, because they were frowned upon in church. That was about the only place I didn't take them.

My favorites were the Marvel Comics. Spider-Man, The Fantastic Four, Iron Man, The Incredible Hulk, Captain America, The Incredible X-Men and others, took me into a world that I loved. In my comics, the bad guys tried, but the good guys always won.

Near the entrance of the Piggly Wiggly, a tall circular rack held my 20-cent treasures. As my mom and sister would stroll the aisles filling the buggy, I would struggle to decide which comic my mom would buy me that week. If I'd been good that week, I got a comic book.

My mom didn't understand my love of comic books, but she did understand that her 20-cent purchase was an investment and savings compared to me walking with her and asking for boxes of Twinkies, Hostess Cupcakes, and every other junk food item that I saw.

Once back home, I would devour my new comic. Losing all track of time, I would read and reread every word. I had, and still have, a special affinity for the ads.

During their heyday from the 1940s through the mid-1970s, comic book ads were like no other advertising. They targeted boys. The ads can best be described as a cross between the patent medicine pitchmen of the late 1800s, and a Saturday Night Live commercial parody.

Only in comic book ads would 25 cents buy you the secret to making girls like you. If you wanted to look like Charles Atlas and be able to stop the bigger guys from kicking sand in your face at the beach, that was an extra 50 cents.

A $1 bill would have real X-ray glasses sent to your mailbox, and an additional dollar would buy you a life-size army tank.

They must have sold a ton of each of these items, because the ads ran unchanged for years.

Comic book trading was also a favorite hobby. Saturdays would find my buddies and me sitting in the middle of one of our rooms with comics stacked and strewn across the floor.

We would begin each session by declaring which comics were off limits and not up for negotiation and which ones would require multiple comics in exchange for one that was available but highly prized.

I even set up a trading arrangement with Mr. Snow and Mr. Walker's barbershop. I wasn't the only kid trading with them, either. This kept the barbershop in a fresh supply of comics for their customers; and many times, I would find a rare jewel in my trade.

The once-ubiquitous comic book is now a rarity. They still publish them, but they're expensive and the artwork is very different than what I grew up on. Kids nowadays have a cell phone or handheld video game with them most of the time but no comic books.

I kept all of my comics. About 30 years ago, I bought items used for their conservation. Each one is in a plastic sleeve and is sorted by name, standing upright in a cardboard box that keeps out most of the light. They sit quietly in a closet, waiting for a day when I feel nostalgic and decide to dig them out.

Every now and then, I'll take out a few and thumb through them. It takes me back to a simpler time that I will always cherish.

If you come across a stack of comics at a yard sale, buy them. You'll enjoy them, I promise.

But a word of warning, the X-ray glasses don't work and the tank is made of cardboard.

A Picky Picker

I was an American Picker before it had a name.

I grew up in a family full of pickers. We just didn't call it that. We called it garage sailing.

The "American Pickers" TV show features a couple of guys from Iowa who travel the country buying old items for resale.

In the 1960s and '70s, my family bought old items, but many times we bought them to use.

My dad's father was a blacksmith, as was his dad before him. Part of running a blacksmith shop required frequenting Saturday-night auctions for items that could be resold or used as a tool to run the business. I cut my picking teeth on auctions in Broken Bow, Oklahoma.

In the late 1960s, my granddad discovered Canton, Texas. Every month he would drive his GMC truck from Ashdown, Arkansas to Canton and barter with the men who set up stands at First Monday Trade Days.

I was about six or seven years old the first time I laid eyes on Canton. For 10 years, until my grandfather's death, I walked behind him and my dad and watched and listened to them converse and haggle with people.

I was like a sponge. Consequently, I learned the art of picking.

Pickers, especially Southern pickers, don't rush. There's a dance that's done before the deal.

You first make friends with the person selling the item or items that you want. You find common ground and chat for a bit. Once you both decide that you like each other pretty well, then you begin to work out a price.

Mike and Frank, the guys on the TV show "American Pickers" use this same approach. The first time I watched them, I knew that they were the real deal. They're a little younger than I am, but they have an eye for many of the same things that I do. Old toys, functional kitchen

160

items, signage, and things that rarely survived are often what they buy.

The other trait they have that I've always tried to offer is fairness. Offer someone a fair price, even if it's more than what they're asking.

After I married and had children, I continued to pick the cities where I lived. I brought home treasures. Some to keep, some to sell for a profit. The money I made went toward more items. And of course I took my children along. They learned the dance of the deal, and they learned fairness.

Being a lifelong picker has provided me an education about how previous generations lived. It has been fascinating.

My family owns and still uses wind-up clocks, tube radios, butter churns, and other items. I enjoy finding something I've never had, buying it, bringing it home, and learning how it works.

My most valued possessions are items that belonged to my family members that they gathered and passed down to me. My grandfather's anvil, his farrier kit, his hat, and leather apron all likely belonged to someone else before he got them. Now, they're mine.

One day, they'll belong to my descendants.

There isn't much else that's more rewarding than searching a flea market, estate sale, garage sale or Craigslist, and finding that needle in a haystack.

Not much else other than passing the picking gene on to the next generation.

Just Call Him 'Cowboy'

"That one was given to a man when he retired from the Illinois Railroad in 1891," said the man who, in his jeans, suspenders and real cowboy hat, looked as if he had just stepped out of a time machine from 1891 himself.

Thin, with the longest white beard I'd seen in awhile, I thought how easy it would be for him to take the stage with ZZ Top and no one would be the wiser.

"How much?" I asked.

"I'd have to have $750 for that one," he said. We were looking at pocket watches he was selling.

I turned the railroad watch over and there was a faded, gold inset of a steam locomotive. Its authenticity was not in doubt. This was an old watch, and it was worn.

"It's key-wound," he said.

"Does it work?" I asked.

He seemed a tad incredulous.

"They all work," he responded.

I glanced through the rest of the glass cases on his table. It looked as if someone had looted part of the Smithsonian. All of his items were valuable.

Most market shows I go to these days aren't selling many antiques anymore. People now sell everything from homemade jerky to gold chain by the inch.

I'd just passed a display where a woman was selling ceramic knives and a cucumber peeler that she guaranteed to be the fastest I would ever own.

"What about this watch?" I asked.

"Oh, that one is special," he said with a smile that shifted his entire beard. "That one was given by Buffalo Bill Cody to one of the Indian chiefs in his Wild West show. I'd have to have $2,000 for that one."

I know a little about Buffalo Bill's Wild West Show. Sitting Bull was with the show for one year in 1885. He left the show and went back to his people, where he was killed by the army during an attempt to arrest him.

If this was a watch given to Sitting Bull by Buffalo Bill Cody, it was worth every bit of $2,000. Probably more.

I'm often skeptical when people tell me stories such as this one, but this fella seemed old school. A straight shooter.

I liked him.

My buddy and I were the only ones looking at the old guy's merchandise. His booth wasn't in the best location. It was against a back wall and not in the highest-traffic area.

"Tell me more about what all you have in your cases," I said.

That request would keep us talking for another 45 minutes. I could tell that he enjoyed sharing his years of acquired knowledge. I also suspected that he had at least 30 years on me and that it wasn't often that someone my age expressed interest in or could converse about pocket watches, small pistols, or old law enforcement memorabilia.

He had a separate glass case full of old badges. There was a marshal's badge from Denver, Colorado. A deputy's badge from New Mexico. Much of the old west was represented there. The case was full. I didn't ask for prices. I knew they would be out of my range.

He showed me watch fobs. He told me the provenance for many, one of which had a storyline that loosely traced all the way back to President Andrew Jackson.

I asked if he made any of the other shows in the area. "Let me check," he said.

He fished a pile of worn cards from his wallet and thumbed through them. He didn't need a calendar on an iPhone. His simple scheduling system seemed to have served him fine for decades.

"I'll be in Dallas at Market Hall on September 25 and 26," he said.

"I've really enjoyed talking with you. I'm John Moore. Tell me your name," I said as we shook hands.

"I could tell you my name," he said, "but no one ever uses it. Just call me 'Cowboy.' Everybody does."

I turned and walked with my friend back through a few more rows of the market, but nothing much else had any appeal for me. I bought some jerky and cheese and purchased 10 chances on a hunting rifle to support a local law enforcement fundraiser.

I passed the lady who was still hawking her cucumber peeler. But I kept thinking about Cowboy.

My buddy said, "You know, he's been around forever. I remember him at the shows in Dallas when I was a teenager."

"Did he look like that back then?" I asked.

"Exactly the same, except for the hair and beard are now gray," he responded.

166

I envy people like Cowboy. Most of us don't love what we do for a living. We work because we have to.

I suspect that he has never considered what he does work. And the coolest thing of all is that they call him "Cowboy."

Just My Type

For those who know me, it's no secret that I enjoy perusing the classifieds for yard or estate sales. But, a recent online visit to the local Craigslist site led to the purchase of a manual typewriter. A 1958 Remington Quiet-Riter, to be exact.

This chapter was written on it.

Some might consider an almost-60-year-old typewriter a nonsensical purchase, considering that desktops, laptops and iPads (the latter typically being my chosen device for writing) are much easier to navigate and correct mistakes.

All of these assertions regarding modern technology are true, but there's just something special about a typewriter, and I decided that I wanted one.

I called the number in the Craigslist ad and an older gentleman answered. I rattled off the typical questions I normally ask regarding anything I'm interested in buying, especially if it's an older item. Does it still work? Any problems with it? What kind of shape is it in?

And, most importantly, why are you selling it?

He explained that when he was in high school in the late 1950s, his grandmother offered to buy him a typewriter if he would take a typing class. He said that he agreed. She bought the typewriter and he took the class, but he said that he had to be honest that he never learned to type very well.

In the '50s, taking typing was not considered very manly. I can only imagine how unmanly it was since I took typing 20 years later in the late 1970s.

In 1977, my buddy Steve and I needed to choose an elective in school. We selected typing class. We picked typing, not because we thought we'd ever really use it much, but because we were 15 and the class was filled with girls.

Once we were in the class, Steve and I quickly realized that typing was no blow-off course.

Typing was difficult. It was especially difficult for two guys in a sea of girls. Mrs. Lewis gave all of the new IBM electric typewriters to them, and Steve and I were relegated to the Underwood manual models leftover from World War II.

Once it became obvious that the girls weren't going to notice us any more in a typing class than they did in study hall, Steve and I decided to make typing a competition.

Anyone who's ever taken typing knows that speed and accuracy are how you're graded. Each day, we would try to outdo the other. Bragging rights became just as important as making a good grade.

I can recall the day that I typed 27 words per minute with no errors. That doesn't sound like much, but I'm telling you, try it today on a manual typewriter and you'll see it's not easy.

Steve and I continued our typing competition and, by year's end, both of us were very proficient.

I would later determine that typing was the most valuable class I've ever taken.

Scarcely a year after typing class, I was accepted in the journalism class to work on the student newspaper and high school annual. The year after that, I was hired at the local radio station, which required the ability to rapidly gather, type and report the news.

The man with the Craigslist ad agreed to meet me in a local grocery store parking lot during my lunch hour. He pulled the typewriter case out of his shiny new truck and placed it on the tailgate. It was quite a contrast: the old typewriter sitting on the back of a modern pickup.

He opened the case and I was very surprised. When he told me that he never really learned to type, I could see why. The Remington looked virtually unused. It was like opening a time capsule.

The original manual was still in the bottom of the case. A woman with a '50s hairdo and wearing clothing from the period smiled at me from the cover as she happily typed.

The keys still had the newness to them. None of the letters or symbols were faded.

We agreed on a price. I paid him, took the typewriter back to work, and later home.

170

I surprised myself with how much I remembered regarding the operation of a manual typewriter. How to feed a sheet of paper, where the lever was to move the carriage back and forth ... it all came back to me.

What I had forgotten was how many of the symbols have been moved. The apostrophe on a typewriter is used by holding down the shift key and punching the number 8. The quotation mark is found by holding the shift key and punching the number 2.

On today's computers, those two symbols are typically found to the right of the colon and semicolon key. On typewriters, the key to the right of the colon and semicolon key includes the @ and ¢ symbols.

The underline key on a modern keyboard is found above the letter P. On a typewriter, you hold the shift key and punch the number 6. Typewriters also have a key for ½ and ¼. Try finding those on a modern keyboard.

I have no idea why these symbols were moved from their original locations, but I had to relearn where they were originally to write this column.

One of the most interesting things I learned about typewriters is that, when adjusted for inflation, they used to cost more than many of today's computers.

On YouTube, I found a TV commercial from 1958 selling my typewriter. It features two girls chatting on the phone. One of them is beaming with glee because her Remington Quiet-Riter was the inspiration for a play she had written, which was about to be staged by the local drama club.

Suddenly, a pitchman appears in the ad, explaining how affordable the new typewriters are. The Remington ranges from $84 to $133.

"Get yours for only $5 down and $1.50 per week, plus carrying charges," he says.

"Carrying charges" is a 1950s term for interest.

I went online and found an inflation converter. If you bought this typewriter in 1958 for $133, that's the equivalent of $1,110.72 in today's money.

Reversing the same calculator, I entered in the $35 I paid the gentleman for his typewriter and discovered that I got a great deal. I paid $4.19 in 1958 money.

I'm appreciative for the great deal he made me, and I'm guessing that his grandmother might have been appreciative that the Remington went to someone who is finally using it.

The truth is, I'm a low-tech kinda guy. My percolator is older than I am, I like old cars better than new ones, and writing this on a typewriter brought me joy and a lot of memories.

It also filled the house with a sound that reminded me of a time when Steve and I tried, but failed, to get the girls' attention.

And Sew It Goes

My friend's mother had passed away and my friend had the unenviable task of sorting through her mom's things. She had decided what she was going to keep, but now she had to price the remaining items, advertise the sale, and then watch as strangers came through her mom's home and took them away.

I've gone to estate sales, yard sales, and garage sales (there are many names for them) all of my life. Some of the best things I've come across and either found a good home for, or kept and used, came from sales such as these.

But this particular sale was different. It was going to change people's lives.

My friend's mom was a quilter. She lived a modest life from what I could tell from her home. I was invited to come ahead of the sale, so I was able to roam freely, my friend by my side, and not have to dodge dozens of other people trying to find a deal for themselves.

The tour of the house was guided. My friend explained what we were seeing. This item her mom had acquired when she was a young woman. That item was bought when my friend and her brother were little. Each thing had a memory attached to it, no matter how common or unique they were.

I bought a hand-crank coffee grinder and one or two other things, but the area I kept coming back to was the room filled with all of the quilting items.

Everything was compartmentalized. The needles and thread had their place, as did the measuring tapes and strips, and the cutters that were used to precisely make quilt squares.

But what I was amazed by was the sheer volume of fabric. There were baskets full of fabric everywhere I looked. Some of it had already been cut and sewn into partial quilt tops, while others were in squares, while others were still large bolts of fabric that had been neatly folded and left for the day that she intended to come back to it for a specific project.

There was a lot of Christmas fabric. A whole lot.

I asked my friend what her mom did with all of her quilts. She said that she gave them away.

She talked about how her mother had made quilts for those in hospice, others who were in need, those she just liked and wanted them to have a quilt, and the many that she made for veterans and children.

If you or anyone close to you has ever quilted, you know how many hours, weeks, and sometimes months it can take to complete a project, based on its complexity.

Quilting used to be part of what most women in a Southern family learned. It was out of necessity. I can remember going to visit my father's parents, and almost always, my dad's mom had a quilt frame set up in the living room and was working on a quilt for someone.

I never paid too much attention to it then, but now I wish that I had. I'd give anything to go back in time and ask my grandmother how she learned to sew and quilt, who the quilts were for, and why she liked making them.

Since my wife quilts, I looked around the room of my friend's mom's home that was filled with all of the quilting materials and had a thought.

"How much for all of the fabric?" I asked.

"All?" she replied. "Yes, everything," I said.

She asked me if I was sure that I wanted to take all of it. After all, I hadn't looked through it with any deep digging, and I'm sure that she knew that me being a guy, I knew virtually nothing about what I was asking to purchase.

She was correct, but I had a feeling that I should buy it all.

We made a deal. I loaded it all up in my car and brought it home.

My wife was both stunned and intrigued. For a moment, I wasn't sure whether I was going to

get a kiss or a tongue-lashing. After she got over
the basket after basket that I had brought in
from the car and stacked in her sewing room, I
sensed that I probably wasn't going to get a kiss
or a tongue-lashing. I'd have to let some time go
by to find out whether I'd made the right
decision.

It took a long time for her to wash and press all
of the different pieces of fabric, sort through the
Christmas pieces, both blocks and partially
finished sections, and arrange all of it in a way
that it seemed organized to her.

The local Methodist church had a quilting
group. My wife heard about it. She attended a
couple of their meetings to see if she liked it.

She did. She loved it.

She would come home from the gatherings and
talk about a quilt that one of the members had
made for hospice, or another who was making
one for someone they knew. My wife went into
detail about someone that a member of the
group knew who everyone felt could use a quilt.
And she talked about the quilts they made for
the children.

Slowly, many of the baskets I brought home from my friend's mom's estate now contain less and less fabric.

And lots of deserving people continue to receive a quilt of their own, thanks to two ladies who never met but shared two things: a selfless love for others and a God-given talent for making quilts.

A Magazine Issue

I have a hard time getting rid of magazines.

I know that I could remove my name and address and donate them to a library or a hospital, but I just know that one day I'll want to dig one back out to reread something.

Even though I've never done that.

My piles of Mother Earth News, Countryside & Small Stock Journal, Smithsonian, Cook's Country, and Guns & Ammo, are growing ever larger.

But magazines are dwindling in number, and many of the best ones ceased publication a long time ago due to a lack of subscribers.

As a kid, it seemed as if every family we knew had a stockpile of National Geographic. They were always lined up chronologically on bookshelves. The oldest issue was quite often an indication of how long a couple had been married or the age of their oldest kid.

My parents subscribed to National Geographic and I liked it. When you only had three TV channels and the Internet didn't exist yet for the general public, that magazine allowed us to see places we'd never visit in person, nor would we learn much about them without that publication. Like every other family, we saved every issue.

I couldn't even venture a guess of how many estate sales I've been to where people were giving away old copies of National Geographic to anyone who would take them.

My mom always made sure that I had a subscription to Boy's Life. I was able to live vicariously through the content of that publication.

And of course my endless supply of comic books was picked up weekly from the rack that stood near the entrance of the Piggly Wiggly. I was more of a Marvel Comics kid than a DC Comics fan, so my acquisitions were mostly The Amazing Spider-Man, The Fantastic Four, Sub-

179

Mariner, Captain Marvel, X-Men, The Avengers, and Iron Man.

God Bless Stan Lee.

There seemed to be a lot of magazines targeting stay-at-home moms back then. Redbook, McCall's, Better Home's and Gardens, and Southern Living, were a few. Moms and their friends would tear out and share recipes and other articles. Many of those can still be found in family recipe boxes and scrapbooks.

As I got older, I used to love The Saturday Evening Post. I'm not old enough to have been around when Norman Rockwell was the cover illustrator, but I did look forward to when it arrived in the mailbox. The stories were always interesting and I learned a lot from reading it.

Life and Look were also great periodicals. Both contained photojournalism at its finest and included compilations of photos of world events, movie stars, and other news of the day.

The large format of each made it possible to see high-quality photos in a larger-than-life format. It's unfortunate that they're no longer available as they were in their heyday. The ability to tell stories with photos is truly a talent.

Today, you simply log on to "The University of Google," as my neighbor calls it, and look at an endless stream of whatever photos you want.

As I aged, I enjoyed other magazines, including The National Lampoon, which was driven by some of the same talented people who went on to be stars on Saturday Night Live, including John Belushi and Chevy Chase. That humor now would be considered politically incorrect, but boy, was it hilarious. I have not found that level of written wit anywhere else since.

People don't seem to subscribe to magazines like they used to. Part of that I'm sure are tight schedules and working long hours, but, like sitting down each morning with my newspaper and percolator coffee, there really is no substitute for some quiet time with the written word.

I keep a stack of the latest magazines on the headboard and by my living room recliner. There are also a few back issues in bookshelves in the living room and in the guest room. Well, OK, there are a lot of them.

But, I am making some progress. I've given some of my older issues to coworkers who said they would also like to read them, and my wife convinced me to recycle some. Not a lot, but some.

Maybe there's a magazine out there that helps people learn how to downsize. If so, I'd subscribe to it.

My Hobby Lobby

I think everyone should have a hobby.

I believe this simply because it's so interesting what each of us finds fascinating.

For some, movies are a hobby. There's a subset of movie lovers who are obsessed with Star Wars.

Pick 10 people on the street and ask them what they think of Star Wars, and you'll likely get nine different answers.

A couple of them will be fanatics and have seen every movie at least three times each. One or two others will be casual fans. Some will have seen one or two of the films but don't understand all of the hype. The tenth guy will tell you that he is a Star Trek fan and that Captain Kirk could easily take out Darth Vader.

What one person latches onto in regard to interests, another couldn't care less about. One man's trash is another man's treasure, as they say.

I grew up in a small Arkansas town where rodeos and roping were part of the fabric of our very existence. Yet, I never had even the least amount of interest in bull riding. It just didn't seem sane to me to get on an angry, 1,500-pound animal for eight seconds for a trophy.

There are plenty of other ways to get trophies, if that's what you like. I have received a number of trophies for bowling, and bowling alleys are air-conditioned and serve beer.

All of us develop interests or hobbies, but watching something on YouTube recently drove home the point of how different we all are and made me wonder how our fascination with certain things develops.

The video I was viewing concerned the rock band, "Queen." Having been a disc jockey during the heyday of what is now referred to as "Classic Rock," Queen and other bands of that era were what I played on the radio during my youth. My fascination for these groups hasn't waned. If anything, it has increased. So, when I ran across a video claiming to include new information about the band, naturally, I clicked on it.

Most of what they mentioned, I already knew. But one thing came out of left field. What surprised me was learning that the group's lead singer, Freddie Mercury, was a philatelist. Now, before you jump to any conclusions about what I'm saying, I'll clarify. A philatelist is a stamp collector.

I paused the video, backed it up, and played that part again. Yep, that's what they said. The lead man of one of the biggest rock bands of the 1970s collected stamps. Granted, he collected them as a younger man, but obviously, his collection is one of note, since it was acquired by a museum two years after his death.

A little online research uncovered that another of my favorite rock icons was also a stamp collector. John Lennon of The Beatles inherited one of his cousins' collections when the pre-Fab Four member was 10 years old.

Unlike Freddie's collection of stamps, which were organized by color and size and were neatly displayed, John's was less presentable, and he had drawn a mustache on the queen. Being a fan of Lennon, that didn't surprise me.

In 2016, both rock stars' collections were displayed together publicly in the United Kingdom.

Is the desire to adopt a specific hobby or two innate, or does it develop because of watching others enjoy certain things?

I think it's a little of both.

As a child, I developed an almost insatiable appetite for comic books. Unlike some kids I knew, I didn't buy comics, read them, and then throw them away. I kept all of mine. I still have them.

I also was (and still am) fascinated by old cars. This was definitely an interest I picked up from my father.

As we would go down the road in my mom's '60 model Buick, my dad would point out the older cars that we passed. I learned all about GM, Ford, Chrysler, and the other major manufacturers. I would later collect classic cars because of the appreciation my father passed down to me.

But, it's always interesting to me what people collect. Sometimes there's a reason for their passion, and sometimes there's not.

Actor Tom Hanks collects typewriters. Singers Rod Stewart and Neil Young are very into model trains, with the latter actually having been part owner of the Lionel Train Company. Allegedly, actor Johnny Depp collects Barbies (don't ask me). And actor Ben Stiller is a Trekkie.

Ben would be the tenth guy I mentioned earlier.

For some, collecting things allows us to hold on to pieces of our past. For others, it allows us to be obsessive but call it something less clinical. Collecting does sound much better than hoarding.

My newest hobby is to collect all of the information that I can on other people's unique hobbies.

I might as well. I'm fairly certain that my bowling trophies and comic books won't be on display in the U.K. after I'm gone.

A Tabled Matter

I was supposed to head straight to the store and back. The garage sale sign I saw not long after leaving home altered my trip just a tad.

I steered my Prius left into the housing addition and followed the arrows. I easily spotted the house. One, because it sat at the top of a small hill, and two, because there were a lot of vehicles in front of it.

It was actually a moving sale, but I use garage sale as a blanket term when discussing any type of sale where people are selling their stuff. This would include estate or moving sales. It's a general term used in the South, much like asking, "What kind of Coke do you want?"

For those of us who frequent garage sales, we know that estate sales and moving sales almost always have better items. We also know that estate sales can be pricey because relatives think grandma's bedroom furniture is worth more than it actually is because they are attached to it. But, deals can be had at moving sales because the sellers don't want to move grandma's bedroom furniture.

The people who were having the sale I stopped at were moving to San Antonio to be near their children. Since I didn't know about the sale ahead of time, I arrived fairly late in the day. That meant most of the good things were gone.

I glanced around the almost-bare display tables at the ashtrays, kitchenware and books, and something caught my eye. It was the legs of one of the display tables. Instead of being the typical folding table legs, these were a pretty, dark wood.

"Is this table for sale?" I asked.

The lady nodded.

"Yes, it is," she said. "There are four chairs in the house that go with it."

The table was covered with a white cloth. I asked if we could remove the cloth so that I could see the tabletop.

After relocating the ashtrays, kitchenware and books to a nearby Rubbermaid folding table, she pulled back the cloth to reveal a beautiful piece of furniture.

I wasn't sure why I instantly liked it so much, but I did. So, I asked to see the chairs.

She took me into her home, which was almost empty, save a china hutch and a few other pieces of furniture. The chairs were in the dining room. I examined them. They also looked great.

We went back outside so that I could look over the table again.

"I almost forgot," she said. "The table has sliders."

I looked for the slit in the center of the table where you would pull it apart to add a table leaf. There wasn't one.

"No," she said. "They're on each end."

She proceeded to pull a hidden leaf from underneath one end of the table. She lifted it slightly and pushed it in. It added a foot to the length.

I wanted this table and chairs.

My wife had recently decided she wanted to replace her round antique dining room table with something rectangular, but we hadn't discussed details.

"How much?" I asked the lady.

She quoted me a price of a few hundred dollars. I called my wife, who agreed to stop working on a quilt and let me come pick her up to come back and take a look.

After seeing it, she liked it, too.

I asked the lady if she knew how old it was, who made it, or where it was made. She didn't. She said that when she and her husband bought the house in 1980, they bought the table and chairs from lady who sold them the home.

She said the lady was quite elderly and that she told them that she had bought the table and chairs when she got married. The lady told her that she and her husband didn't have much money, but she wanted one nice thing for her home to start her marriage. She had picked this.

We loaded the five pieces carefully into our truck and took it home.

I began to inspect the chairs for any problems but found nothing major. I crawled underneath the table. I almost missed it, but something caught my eye. It was a sticker with a drawing of a Victorian-looking woman staring at a piece of furniture. Above the drawing were the words, "Consider H. Willett Inc. Product. Manufacturer of Fine Furniture. Louisville, Kentucky."

Below the drawing were the words, "All Walnut."

I could find almost nothing on the web, except that the furniture company was in business from 1929 until 1962, and that they were known for quality furniture at a reasonable price.

After World War II, their furnishings were so popular that people had to wait up to one year to have theirs delivered.

The legs on a couple of the chairs were a little loose, so I took them to a local antique furniture repair store. The man took one look at them and asked if I had any idea what I had. I told him that I did not.

He told me that the company only made the walnut pieces for three years in the 1930s. He also told me that the table and chairs were quite rare and valuable.

My wife and I were pleasantly surprised.

I came back later to pick up the chairs and reunite them with the rest of the set.

We've had them for a few years now and we use them daily. On the table, my wife lays out quilt pieces, we play Scrabble, and we share meals.

We don't consider ourselves the owners of this table and chairs. We are the current stewards.

Whoever gets it after our days with them are done, will get the story that goes with it. And they'll have to promise to take extra good care of the one thing a bride chose to put in her home at the beginning of her marriage during America's Great Depression.

The TV Guide

There were three TV channels when I was a kid. The signals of two of them were reliable. The third was iffy. If there was a storm, CBS probably wasn't going to have a picture.

Nestled in the southwest corner of Arkansas, my hometown was not near any of the television towers. Radio stations were plentiful, but the closest television stations were in Shreveport. Little Rock and Dallas had stations, but the signals didn't reach us.

So, we subsisted on ABC, CBS, and NBC. This limited access to programming would seem like a TV diet designed by Jenny Craig compared to today's ability to access shows on cable, satellite, and the internet. But, 50 years ago, there were plenty of shows worth watching.

Television in the 1960s and '70s was the gathering place for Americans. Since there were far fewer programs then, virtually everyone met up – same time, same channel – to see what was happening next.

If television was the gathering place, then *TV Guide was* the road map to get there. *TV Guide* began as a regional publication in the northeast in the late 1940s. Not many people had a TV then, but by the mid-'50s, a lot of people did.

In 1953, *TV Guide* debuted nationally for 15¢ a copy. Lucille Ball and her newborn son, Desi Arnaz Jr., were on the cover. Lucy still holds the record for most cover appearances.

Moving shows around the schedule isn't anything new. When I was young, networks were constantly shifting the day and time of our favorite programs. Since there was no internet, we had to have a way to find out when *Bonanza, The Twilight Zone, Lost In Space, Star Trek, The Beverly Hillbillies, Columbo, All In The Family, Sanford and Son,* and other series were going to be on.

The arrival of *TV Guide* in the mailbox was an event. We not only wanted to make sure that we didn't miss our shows, we also wanted to see who made the cover.

Much like the celebrity magazines of today, if someone made the cover of *TV Guide*, that was a sign that their star was either rising or that they had already arrived in the TV business.

Each issue, which was the size of a *Reader's Digest,* began with Saturday's show listings and ran through the following Friday. So, if the *TV Guide* wasn't in the mail by Thursday, concern would set in. If it didn't arrive by Friday, general panic would set in.

In addition to show listings, the weekly magazine also had editorial content and ads. If a program was featured in the Close-Up section, that was an indication that the editorial staff felt that it had significance. They would write about why the show mattered and what we could expect if we watched it.

The Cheers and Jeers section was just what it sounds like. Cheers for things on TV they liked, and jeers for what they didn't.

The TV networks would buy ads to promote shows that were doing marginally well or needed a boost. Programs such as *60 Minutes, The Jeffersons, Happy Days, and The Rockford Files* didn't need much advertising support. But, shows such as *Manimal, The Big Bow Wow,* and

194

Cop Rock, did. As you can probably guess, the ads didn't help the latter.

The *Fall Preview Issue* was the issue everyone always looked forward to. It included information on new and returning shows. To give you some idea of how much it meant, many families would keep this issue and not toss it like the others.

Our *TV Guide* resided on the small table next to my dad's chair. You were welcome to pick it up and take it somewhere else and read it but forgetting to put it back meant that you got to hear your first, middle, and last names called out fairly loudly.

Not only did my dad rely on the *TV Guide* to decide whether we were watching *The Red Skelton Show* or *The Wonderful World of Disney*, he relied on it to get a crossword puzzle fix. The puzzle appeared at the back of the magazine and included the names of television stars and their shows.

At one point in the early '70s, nearly 20 million people bought *TV Guide*. But, the advent of cable TV made it difficult to print a comprehensive list of channels for everyone. Even my small town eventually got a cable company. The networks could appear on one channel for us, but on a different channel for the folks in the next town over. The same problem arose when people could choose satellite over cable. The channels were different there than on cable, or on the channels people still received on an antenna.

Consequently, fewer and fewer people subscribed to *TV Guide.* It seemed to go the way of S&H Green Stamps.

Honestly, I don't remember when my family stopped getting *TV Guide,* but on a recent trip to my parents' house, I ran across a few that they had saved, including some old fall previews and one from 1978 that featured interviewer David Frost and former president Richard Nixon on the cover. No one could come up with a good reason why the Nixon copy was kept.

I was surprised to learn that *TV Guide* is still around. Fewer than 2 million people buy it now, but it's available not only in a printed version (which is now the size of a regular magazine), but can also be downloaded to your computer, phone, or tablet. It even has a YouTube channel.

If you kept some of your old *TV Guide* issues, you might want to dig them out. Some are quite valuable as collector's items. A copy of the first issue with Lucy and her son on the cover would bring quite a bit. Likely, enough to buy a lot of really nice TVs.

CHAPTER EIGHT – THE GREAT OUTDOORS AND OTHER QUASI-MANLY PURSUITS

A Man Cave Man

I had a man cave before it was called that.

For eons, men have had a space they called their own. A place to get away. This space has been called a number of different things, but the purpose was the same. When the pressures of their time reached an unacceptable level, they could escape.

One hundred years ago, when America was primarily an agrarian society, men had a barn. There, they could retreat to a day of taking care of the livestock, the blacksmithing chores, and other tasks. They were actually working, which gave them the perfect excuse to head out back.

The conversation probably went something like this:

Ma: "Pa, all 10 of the children need new shoes, and we don't have enough egg money in the jar to pay for them. What are you expectin' to do about it?"

Pa: "I'm going to the barn for a spell to think on it, Ma. Don't hold supper fer me. I might be awhile."

I suspect that the cave man used a similar approach; just a different location.

Cave Woman: "Grogg, you and your buddies just ate the last of the mastodon. What do you propose that I feed the children?"

Cave Man: "Me go to other cave over mountain to make plan. Don't wait up. Ugh."

Over the last 50 years or so, lots of men have had a workshop. For many, this started as a place away from the house where they could work on projects or repair things.

Out of necessity, most guys knew a little about a lot. They had to. Very few families had the money to pay someone to repair everything that broke, so they were taught by their fathers how to fix a lamp, lawnmower, or just about anything else.

Their workshops also gave men the perfect place to escape.

Wife: "Honey, the Johnsons just called and want to know if we want to come over and watch a slideshow of their trip to Omaha. Do you want to go?"

Husband: "Can't do it, honey. Have to go to the shop and fix a broken lamp and lawnmower."

In 2003, we moved to the country. There was an unfinished shop on the property. The slab and cinder block walls were there, but that was all. After rounding up a group of relatives and friends who worked for beer, I was able to complete the 15×20 structure and set up my very first workshop.

First, I acquired all of the workshop essentials. I bought a 55-inch, high-definition plasma TV, a refrigerator, radio, and charcoal grill. Later, as the budget allowed, I also bought some tools.

A few years after finishing and moving everything into my shop, I started hearing the term "Man Cave."

According to the Merriam-Webster Dictionary, a man cave is: "A room or space designed according to the taste of the man of the house to be used as his personal area for hobbies and leisure activities."

That has a nice ring to it, doesn't it?

There is now a cottage industry of businesses that sells things just for man caves. Everything from neon signs, to complete bars and liquor cabinets, to home theater systems.

When we built my shop, I had no idea that it would one day morph into a man cave. But, it has worked out.

I've even acquired new friends because of it. My new buddy Grogg is bringing over some mastodon later to throw on the charcoal grill.

Camping Can Get Tents

Man spent thousands of years in the wilderness, scrounging for food, dodging danger and searching for a safe precursor to toilet paper. After finally conquering agriculture, domesticating many animals, and inventing Charmin, Americans now spend millions each year to go back into the woods.

In movies and on TV, camping is presented as being utopia. Even medication ads for older, less functional men seem to indicate that a pill and a pup tent are all a happy couple needs.

But the truth is, for most people, camping is miserable.

I can't remember one camping trip in my entire life that didn't include rain, sunburn, mosquitoes, chiggers, rain, fire ants, burnt food, or, don't forget, rain.

When I was a preteen, my parents bought a pop-up camper. Typical of most affordable early 1970s small RV's, it was pulled behind the family car (in our case, a Buick) to a campsite completely devoid of modern conveniences.

Arriving at the campground, my dad would proceed to grunt as he worked to level the camper. Then a handle, that was reminiscent of a Model T crank, would appear and be placed in the side of the camper, then turned until the unit stretched upward, outward, and into place. This scene was followed by my father collapsing.

The inside of the camper had a small central area where a Coleman Stove sat. Each end contained thin foam mattress pads for sleeping.

Our activities included sweating, itching, being bored, and not sleeping.

When the trip was over, which seemed more like parole from a 10-year prison sentence, we would load back into the Buick and head home;

dreaming of Captain Kangaroo, Cap'n Crunch, central air conditioning and normalcy.

When my childhood camping years came to a close, I swore that I'd never go camping again.

Fast-forward to marriage.

My first wife announces one day that we were going to take our then two small sons camping. Never mind the fact that we owned no camping gear, one son was barely out of diapers, and that I hated camping.

After purchasing enough camping gear to put each Walmart stockholder's kids through college, off we went to a campsite, once again completely devoid of modern conveniences.

Not being able to afford the traditional pop-up camper, we set up our new tent, stove and the rest of our campsite.

A few hours later, it began to rain. And it rained some more. And then some more. It rained so hard that you couldn't see anything.

And then it began to flood. Lightning danced around us.

The only thing preventing our tent, us, and everything else from floating away were the tent stakes.

I finally convinced her that for our safety, we had to leave.

Putting her and the two boys into our new minivan, I pulled the tent stakes, left everything inside the tent, wadded it into a ball, and shoved it into the back of the vehicle.

I got into the driver's seat. When the water finally stopped pouring out of my ears, I could hear her asking me, "So, what are we going to do now?"

It was a quiet ride back to my parents, which was the closest place from the campground that we could seek shelter.

When I awoke the next morning, the sun was out and it was a beautiful day. I searched for a good place on top of which I could lay the tent, sleeping bags, and everything else to dry.

Fortunately, my parents' pop-up camper, which hadn't been used in 20 years, was available.

The Fix Is In

I grew up in a family who fixed things. We fixed things because we didn't have the money to pay someone else to fix them. As a result, I was taught a little about a lot when it came to everyday items.

Things used to be made simply. Consequently, in most cases you could fix most items yourself. A fan, for example, was rudimentary. A housing, blade, electric motor, and a plug was pretty much all there was to one. The older fans had a small oil port in the back where you would add 3-In-One Oil to keep the shaft moving smoothly.

Toasters were basic. A nice, shiny housing contained a spring mechanism, a heating element, and adjustments for how dark you wanted your bread.

Lawnmower engines were basic. Air, a spark and fuel were all you needed to crank and mow. The ability to fix your own things isn't as common as it once was, but it's still the case more often than not. These days, most folks just don't learn how.

Labor Day weekend, my pickup and two of my lawnmowers decided that it was a great time to break down. I don't know about at your house, but most of the time when the plumbing, air conditioning, or something else that we've grown to believe is a necessity breaks down at our house, it seems to happen on a holiday weekend when all of the repairmen are charging triple time.

I got about halfway to work Friday morning when the front right wheel began doing its best impression of a Halloween banshee. I limped it home and parked it in the yard, got in my Prius and headed on to work.

I am by no stretch a mechanic, but I can work on vehicles to some degree. My grandfathers and my dad all taught me that if I maintain a car or truck by following the owner's manual, a vehicle will last a long time. They were correct. When my grandfathers passed away, their vehicles both drove and looked like new.

All three men taught me how to work on engines. This ability and knowledge has saved me a lot of money over the years.

So, while at work on Friday, I mapped out my Labor Day weekend. I would assess what was wrong with the truck and repair it if possible. But first, I would mow the yard. We have a fairly large yard, so we have multiple lawnmowers. The John Deere zero-turn covers more area and mows faster, but the smaller riding mower we've had forever still runs, so I keep it as a backup.

So, first thing Saturday morning, I head out to mow. The zero-turn wouldn't start.

What happened next is something every man has experienced. The last domino fell. The only functioning riding mower I had left decided to disintegrate underneath me. As I made a circle in the front yard, my John Deere model L118 began riding rough. As I completed the circle, I discovered why it was riding rough. I passed one of the lawnmower's wheels lying in the yard.

The John Deere was determined that he had breathed his last, but I was not going to let him go. I was almost certain that no lawnmower shop would be open on a holiday weekend; but even if they were, I wasn't going to pay triple time.

Passing my dead truck in the front yard, I limped my lawn tractor to my shop where I began to assess the damage. It wasn't good.

The wheel that had come off was part of the blade deck. It is a welded piece, which means

207

you have to weld it back on. A further inspection revealed that one of the deck brackets, which holds the blade deck in place underneath the riding mower, had cracked away from the deck and was holding on by a thread. The rest of Saturday and half of Sunday, I spent cleaning, grinding, and welding on that lawn tractor. After many hours, lots of sweat, and exhaustion, I fixed it.

I then moved my focus back to the zero-turn. Cleaning the battery posts and removing a chunk of wood that had wedged itself between one of the blades and the blade deck had me zero-turning in no time.

Sure, my John Deere L118 lawn tractor has 432.5 hours on it. Sure, it fouls a plug every now and then. Sure, one of the guide wheels broke off and I had to work to weld it all back together. But, that's OK.

My truck had an inexpensive solenoid go out. An easy fix.

We now live in a disposable society, but it doesn't have to be that way.

Ohm Improvement

I remember when VCRs came out. It seemed
that no one over the age of 27 knew how to stop
the clock from flashing 12:00.

It was such a simple fix that I never understood
why the adults couldn't figure it out.

Even after I showed them how to fix the clock,
they still couldn't grasp it.

The same was true for programming the thing to
record "Columbo," "The Andy Griffith Show,"
or any of the other programs that grown-ups
couldn't live without.

I always knew that if the electricity went out, I
would be summoned to reprogram the unit.

It was a small thing, but it just seemed odd.
Then, home computers came out. The people
who had the money to buy them couldn't
operate them. That wasn't true in every case, but
it was true fairly often.

They wanted the technology, but either they
feared it, didn't understand it, or just flat didn't
want to learn anything new.

That last one I'm finally starting to grasp.

Not too long ago, the heating and cooling system in our home finally went out. It was pushing 20 years old, so that's pretty good. I almost choked on the price, but hey, it's Texas. You don't go without air-conditioning in the Lone Star State.

Where I drew the line was the controller the guy was replacing in the hallway. He began to tell me how I could program it for a morning phase, a midday phase, an afternoon phase, a vacation phase, etc.

Hold it. No. Just no. All I wanted was an on/off, hotter/colder, thermostat.

The older unit that was in the house when we bought it had a programmable thermostat, and I had to get someone younger than 27 to figure it out so that we wouldn't burn up or freeze.

"But, you paid for the Turbo 9000 Climate Controller Module," he said.

I don't care if I paid for a Prius. I just want on/off, hotter/colder.

So, he left and came back with exactly what I asked for. Later, when the thing stopped working and the screen went blank, I found out that it runs on triple A batteries.

I can't win for losing.

Speaking of a Prius, I own one. Granted, these cars are pretty amazing feats of engineering. They get about 50 miles to the gallon. But, why do all of the things I need as a driver have to require a degree from MIT?

After we bought the one we have now, I was told that I could program some buttons on the rearview mirror to open and close the garage door. After reading the instructions and watching a couple of videos on YouTube, I not only had not programmed the buttons to open the garage door, I had completely confused our cat, who didn't know whether I was coming home or leaving.

I finally gave up and stuck the garage door opener back on the sun visor.

To keep up with TV technology, I replaced our old set with a new Smart TV. I quickly discovered that the TV was now the only smart thing left in the living room.

After unfurling a schematic that looked like it came from the space shuttle, I finally figured out how to get a picture on the thing. But, I was faced with an array of squares on the screen that asked me if I wanted to watch something on cable, the Internet, the DVD player, or some other source.

I added the new remote control to the pile of the other four that sit on the table between our chairs.

Music also used to be much easier. If you wanted some, you turned on a radio. Now, you have the local stations, satellite radio, Pandora, iHeart Radio, and so on, all of which can be listened to through my phone. That is, if I could remember what the passwords are to get in and turn them on.

For power outages, we bought a new generator. I used to have a smaller one on wheels that I'd drag around the house to plug in when the juice went out. It was simple. If it had gas and oil, you turned a key and on it came. You plug it in, turn it on, and your wife's curling iron works.

Simple enough, right?

The new generator is large and has its own pad. I liked that idea very much. Then the guy who sold it to us lifted a lid and started showing me how to program it.

Wait. Something else I have to program? Why do I need to program a generator? Turns out, that for maintenance purposes, they need to come on and go off by themselves once a week. Fortunately, this thing doesn't require triple A batteries.

All of this new technology is exhausting. I'd just like to go in the house and watch Columbo and Andy Griffith.

And I will. As soon as I figure out how.

CHAPTER NINE – THANK YOU FOR YOUR SERVICE

Soldiering On

I sat near the front of the auditorium. I was the fourth to speak, so I wanted to be as near the podium as possible. But, I sat in the section to the left. The center area was for the veterans.

There were only two.

It was the 74th memorial service for the Camp Fannin Association, and it was held at UT Health Northeast, which now occupies the site of one of the largest military training facilities of the Second World War. I was asked to give part of the welcome.

I did some quick math in my head. If these two men were 17 or 18 when they were at Camp Fannin between 1943 and 1946, these two gentlemen are 90 or older.

I'm a huge fan and student of history, but there was much I learned that day about Camp Fannin and about all of those who were at the camp to train before they were sent to the front lines to defend our country.

For many, it was a one-way trip.

After the Japanese attacked Pearl Harbor in 1941, the men and women of what former news anchor Tom Brokaw appropriately called "The Greatest Generation" mobilized and geared up in very short order to fight for our freedom and our future.

Factories that made automobiles were quickly converted to build Jeeps, planes, and other needed mechanized tools of war.

Women left the home to work the jobs that were vacated by the men who enlisted. Many of those men who enlisted came to Camp Fannin.

Just as the factories were converted for the war effort, the United States government took 14,000 acres near what is now the area on Highways 271 and 155, and in six months, built 600 barracks, a hospital, roads, and all of the other things needed for a training facility for soldiers.

A former sheriff was the featured speaker at the memorial, and he showed photos and shared many of the stats about Camp Fannin.

A small many as 40,000 men at once were at Camp Fannin, he said.

Estimates put the total number of men who trained at the U.S. Army Infantry Replacement Training Center at around 200,000.

In 1944, 16,000 soldiers were marched from Camp Fannin to downtown Tyler. The march circled the town square and then made its way back to the camp.

At that time, it was one of the largest military marches in the country.

I thought about what that must've been like to witness. Before television, events such as this one would've been available as a photograph in the newspaper or a radio report. It had to be quite amazing to see.

Many of those who are from the Tyler area who were here during the short time that Camp Fannin was here are now gone. So, all that remains of events such as the march are the photographs.

There were other photos of a wartime Christmas. What appeared to be one of the barracks had the letters, "Merry Christmas" sitting on the roof with lights to illuminate them.

There were many pictures of military generals standing and inspecting troops. They were watching the enlisted men training, firing weapons, and in one photo, pushing a Jeep out of the mud.

As J.B. pointed out, the enlisted men always got the grunt work. I'm sure they still do.

As I listened, I glanced back at the two Camp Fannin veterans. They were quiet and attentive. I tried to imagine what was going through their minds. They were seeing photos from this period in their lives. Did they remember when these were taken? Were they there for any of the events we were seeing?

Americans weren't the only ones here in East Texas at that time. German prisoners of war were also held at the camp.

Just two days before the memorial service, the daughter of a lieutenant who had served at the camp donated a large model ship built by a German POW to the Camp Fannin Association.

The German built the model from things he had available. The ship is on loan to UT Health and is on display there.

For a few years, East Texas was the destination for thousands: some who came willingly, and others who were captured and held. But, each person was someone's son, brother, or husband. The Camp Fannin Association works to keep their sacrifice and the memory of what they did alive. We owe it to those who came before us to support their efforts and to learn our own community's history.

I was honored to be a part of the memorial and to learn more about the thousands of heroes who called Tyler home as they trained to put their lives on the line for their fellow man and future generations.

Only a few are still with us. This day there were two.

About
John Moore

John Moore is a syndicated columnist and an award-winning voice and radio personality.

To learn more about John or purchase additional books, visit his website at:

TheCountryWriter.com.

Made in USA - Crawfordsville, IN
76303_9781696793629
02.15.2020 1051